C A B I N

F E V E R

CABIN FEVER
RUSTIC STYLE COMES HOME

RACHEL CARLEY

AN ARCHETYPE PRESS BOOK

SIMON & SCHUSTER EDITIONS

CONTENTS

ROUGHING IT: RUSTIC STYLE REVISITED

110

CATALOGUE: THE COMPANY STORE

182

OUT OF THE WOODS

THE ROOTS OF RUSTIC

William Distin, a well-known architect in New York's Adirondack Mountains in the early 1900s, once designed a bark-covered vacation lodge for an affluent client, who promptly set sail for Europe. A few months later, as the story goes, he wired home: "Will arrive Thursday. Please buy dishes and have roast lamb for dinner." Distin reportedly was ready with the house, the meal, and a dining table set with crystal and monogrammed silver.

Cabin fever to the extreme? Perhaps, but the improbabilities and occasional excesses in the country's long-standing romance with the wild outdoors are what make the history of rustic retreats so fascinating and truly American. The fashion for remote hotels, hunting lodges, clubs, and private vacation "camps" built of rugged natural materials began in earnest after the Civil War, when the pressures of a newly industrialized society fed a desire for variety and escape. The conceit of "roughing it" in log or stone buildings (often furnished with silver and crystal) originated among the affluent Victorian social set, which had the time and the means to travel long distances. Within a short period, however, families of more modest means were building their own woodland retreats for just a few hundred dollars.

The log buildings typically favored for wilderness camps and western ranches were closely associated with a log cabin myth that romanticized the hardy outdoor life of American pioneers and identified the cabin with a democratic frontier spirit and the dream of the good life. The nineteenth-century obsession with the wilderness was in fact closely linked to a fascination with the frontier experience and its rapid disappearance. At the time of the Louisiana Purchase in 1803, the West was still uncharted territory and America's natural plenitude seemed inexhaustible. But the opening of the West brought a steady stream of exploitation, first by the fur trade and then by intense logging. Along with the loss of woodlands came the decimation of Native American populations and the settlement of formerly remote areas along rapidly expanding railroad lines. The passing of the frontier was declared a reality by the eleventh U.S. Census, conducted in 1890, which claimed that a true line of wilderness no longer existed in America.

Soon after a group of Boston friends adopted a mountain farm as their Adirondack retreat and named it Putnam Camp in the 1870s, they added a simple wood-frame building called the Stoop. This rustic open-air parlor has remained virtually unchanged.

The quintessential Gilded Age retreat in the Adirondacks was a self-sufficient estate of many structures now known as the Great Camp. Shown at his three-story boathouse (opposite), Adolph Lewisohn reportedly spent more than $2 million on Prospect Point, the twenty-eight-building compound he began on Upper Saranac Lake in 1903. Another Great Camp, Santanoni, on Newcomb Lake, included a working farm, a separate service complex, and a waterside lodge (background above), built about 1888. Boating—in full dress, of course—was de rigueur.

Going Home, to the Wilderness

The importance of connecting to nature in the face of industrial progress underscored many aspects of nineteenth-century life. Nature's place in humanity's spiritual regeneration was already a pervasive theme in contemporary philosophy and literature. "In the wilderness we return to reason and faith," wrote Ralph Waldo Emerson, who led a group of like-minded luminaries to a campsite retreat called Philosophers' Camp on Follensby Pond in the Adirondacks as early as 1858. The Adirondacks, the Green and White Mountains of Vermont and New Hampshire, and the mountains and canyons of the Far West were also early destinations for artists and photographers, who brought their stupendous beauty to the attention of the American public.

In the race to document the receding wilderness, many artists became conservationists. The painter Thomas Moran joined the Hayden Survey in 1871 when it undertook the first official documentation of Yellowstone Canyon. He garnered widespread support for making Yellowstone the first national park the next year, becoming known as the father of the American park system. A well-known artists' colony thrived in Keene Valley in the heart of the Adirondacks, where a 2.8 million-acre state park (now six million acres) was created in 1892. The region was a magnet for such noted landscape artists as Asher Durand, Winslow Homer, and Thomas Cole, the latter considered the first American to express Emerson's ideas with a paintbrush.

By the turn of the century, public transportation made travel possible for a broader cross section of Americans, who developed a protective attitude toward the natural wonders they were seeing for the first time. The railroads, which started the first major concession areas in the national parks and were the biggest boosters of the American West, actively promoted tourism and dude ranching. The vogue for hiking and mountaineering led to an increase in the number of national park visitors from 69,000 in 1908 to 335,000 in 1915. The benefits were widely apparent. "Thousands of tired, nerve-shaken, over-civilized people are beginning to find out that going to the mountains is going home; that wilderness is a necessity; and that mountain parks and reservations are useful not only as fountains of timber and irrigating rivers, but as fountains of life," commented Sierra Club founder John Muir at the time.

ACCOMMODATIONS FOR NATURE LOVERS

Newly accessible, the nation's fabulous natural areas were the logical locales for rustic lodges and hotels, which held precisely the same romantic appeal as private woodland camps. At the start of the 1900s, the rustic image was adopted for national park hotels and became the foundation for a clever national marketing strategy. Most of the early park hotels were in fact built by competing railroad companies hoping to attract business to their new lines. They made natural wonders available to all and offered the added novelty of luxury accommodations in a wilderness setting.

No building, for example, could be more worthy of the extravagant scale and rugged beauty of Wyoming's Rocky Mountain wilderness than Old Faithful Inn, conceived by the Northern Pacific Railroad as a showcase hotel for the Upper Geyser Basin at Yellowstone National Park. Built and expanded over a twenty-five-year period beginning in 1903, the seven-hundred-foot-long structure was one of the largest and most expensive national park hotels of its day (costing more than $400,000) and remains one of the most significant examples of rustic architecture in America. The architect Robert Reamer's dark, brooding facades, log cladding, and rough-hewn details represent an early attempt to project a wild frontier image that captures the essence of the landscape and pays homage to its beauty. Novel and exciting, the hotel was a success as soon as it opened its doors in 1904 and proved as much a curiosity as the sheer rock cliffs, waterfalls, and hydrothermal wonders of the 2.2 million-acre park itself.

Old Faithful Inn's consciously rustic design incorporated a steep roof (right top) and gnarled log staircases (right bottom). Changing levels in the ninety-two-foot-high lounge (opposite) are intended to recreate an actual woodland experience, encouraging guests to pause for views as they climb and descend.

Nothing sold rooms and tickets like wilderness. To exploit this theme, railroad architects created a powerful rustic hotel style defined by a bold use of natural materials and an exaggerated scale that celebrated the buildings' natural settings. Charles Whittlesey's 1905 El Tovar, a magnificent pile of stone, rough-hewn logs, and wood shingles, represented the Santa Fe Railroad's bid to draw travelers to one of the nation's most awesome natural wonders by providing a destination resort of architectural distinction at the Grand Canyon in Arizona.

In hotels like these, cavernous lobbies and dining rooms captured the eye and the imagination with massive wood-burning fireplaces, gnarled staircases, and mock-primitive details. To complete the effect, furnishings included down-home hickory and wicker, along with suitably "honest" Stickley Craftsman pieces of rawhide and oak and Indian pottery and rugs that made exotic reference to the western frontier. The quest for originality often resulted in a confusing mix of popular styles of the day, but it produced hotels unique in their exuberance and spirit. The best became destinations in themselves—although none ever completely upstaged its surroundings.

Promotional literature for the El Tovar (opposite) called the remote Arizona hotel's eclectic style "Swiss chalet and Norman villa." Another rustic retreat, Gilbert Stanley Underwood's Ahwahnee Hotel (left), built of boulders and concrete in 1927, acknowledges the beauty of California's Yosemite Valley without trying to compete.

RETREATS FOR CAPITALISTS AND COWPOKES

In the days before air conditioning, summer resorts also grew up in cool mountain and lake areas located along rail lines and targeted by real estate speculators. The Adirondacks and New England mountains drew families from Boston, Philadelphia, and New York. Mountain hamlets such as Blowing Rock and Linville in western North Carolina were a refuge from the hot city pavements of Nashville, Charlotte, and Birmingham. The Great Lakes wilderness spawned private hunting lodges, clubs, and resorts for the barons of industry from Toledo, Detroit, and Minneapolis. Pasadena capitalists developed rustic resorts on Lake Tahoe for California's fashionable set. That most lodges and retreats were difficult to reach only underscored the owners' financial resources and capacity for leisure pursuits. The Ohio industrialists sharing the 1898 fishing camp Wa Wa Sum on the Au Sable River in Michigan traditionally left Toledo on Thursday nights. Met by their private guides at 4:30 the next morning, they were paddled some twenty miles upstream so that they could fish their way down to camp in time for breakfast.

Incorporating bark and log siding, exposed knotholes, gnarled details, and twiggy furniture, the woodsy design favored for these camps was very much a product of the time. Rough timber and stone were in obvious harmony with their surroundings, and it was only logical to use local materials and artisans in remote areas. Mainly, however, rustic was fashionable. Although the log cabin itself was associated with the winning of the West, such rustic elements as decorative gables were modeled in part after eighteenth- and nineteenth-century English picturesque designs. The pervasive chalet style was introduced to America by English pattern books in the 1820s, then picked up at midcentury by such American tastemakers as Alexander Jackson Downing. The rage for rustic buildings later in the century coincided with a European revival of the "piquant," or picturesque, alpine vernacular of Germany, Switzerland, and France and was spread across America by influential professional periodicals from England and Germany. These, according to a speaker at the 1895 convention of the American Institute of Architects, "furnished the sole inspiration of nearly every architectural office in the land."

The famed Adirondack camp Sagamore, begun in 1896 by William West Durant—considered the father of the rustic Great Camps—had rather basic furnishings in the main lodge, including folding camp chairs and a chandelier wrapped in fishing net (above). The chalet design (opposite top) was influenced by alpine buildings in Europe. After purchasing the camp, Alfred G. Vanderbilt (far right in the first sled) added numerous amenities for lavish entertaining. Log siding and the original red trim (opposite bottom) enhance the quaint effect.

American Victorian taste was often more enthusiastic than discriminating, and rustic soon took off in every imaginable direction as Americans added their own twists. Formality may have reigned in fashionable seaside colonies such as Newport, Rhode Island, but there was something about the woods that made people let loose. The railroad scion and real estate entrepreneur William West Durant is credited with introducing the prototypical rustic Great Camp in the Adirondacks in the 1870s with his Camp Pine Knot on Raquette Lake. A tourist attraction in its own time, this extravaganza of cedar bark and log featured separate buildings for eating, cooking, and sleeping, as well as a floating cabin with four bedrooms, a kitchen, a bath, and running water. One later Adirondack camp included a bark replica of the Parthenon, and still another boasted a pyramid-shaped "Egyptian" tent complete with hieroglyphics. On twelve thousand acres bordering the shores of Lake Superior, Louis Graveraet Kaufman in 1919 built his rustic estate, Granot Loma. From a manmade harbor to a fifty-room main lodge, the retreat encompassed an eight-bedroom guest house, an eight-car garage, staff quarters for twenty-eight, and steel-vaulted his-and-hers wine cellars (quickly finished just before Prohibition).

In addition to exotic foreign influences of the day (the Frederick Vanderbilts dressed their servants in Japanese kimonos), rustic lodges typically mixed in elements from all the same styles popular in suburban America after the Civil War: the Queen Anne, the Shingle Style, the Colonial Revival, the chalet mode, and Craftsman design. Furnishings were equally eclectic. Japanese accessories, Windsor chairs, factory-made cottage furniture, rough-hewn pieces fashioned by guides and caretakers, and dead animals filled every room. Indian artifacts peddled as rustic decorations in railroad souvenir shops also found their way into countless homes. Stickley and Mission furniture was favored too, but only because it was fashionable—not because customers followed the philosophy of the Craftsman movement, which rejected the same Gilded Age excess that many early woodland camps celebrated.

Bark-covered bunks were a novelty at William West Durant's Camp Pine Knot in the Adirondacks (opposite bottom), while at Granot Loma twigwork spun a web over a guest cottage (opposite top). The Michigan estate's extravagant decor included hand-carved logs (left top) and bedsteads of gnarled tree roots (left bottom).

A Refuge from Routine

By the 1930s, the national income tax and the onset of the Great Depression had spelled the end for America's most extravagant wilderness getaways. At the same time, however, the Works Progress Administration initiated many reforesting projects and in 1937, at the height of the Depression, produced the rustic Timberline Lodge, tucked into the southern brow of snow-crested Mount Hood in Oregon. The timber-frame mountain hotel, stretching 360 feet along a rocky ridge six thousand feet above sea level, was an ambitious public project—Oregon's largest WPA building and one of the largest of Franklin D. Roosevelt's New Deal constructions.

During the same period, federal and state governments began leasing permanent building sites in forest and park lands and selling timber at cheap stumpage rates. Wilderness living thus grew even more within reach of the average American. "Here is the real big opportunity to live in a forest paradise on land leased for a nominal sum," claimed the author of a 1937 pattern book entitled *Camps, Log Cabins, Lodges and Clubhouses*. "Our Government will grant you the opportunity," he added. "You make the most of it."

Although wilderness living may not quite be considered patriotic duty, the impulse to retreat to nature remains universal. The rustic tradition, as it did a century ago, still offers people a refuge from the routine patterns of daily life, a connection to place, and a feeling of sanctuary and quiet. Natural materials and regional furnishings establish physical surroundings with a joy and dignity suiting the landscapes of meadow, mountain, and water that draw us into nature's world. Cabin fever is in the air.

At Oregon's Timberline Lodge, Works Progress Administration carvings such as a wise owl (right), inspired by Indian ethnology and local fauna, were conceived by the Portland decorator Margery Hoffman Smith. Heavy pegged arches (opposite) were intended to convey a sturdy "pioneer" look for the western hotel.

THE LOG CABIN LOOK

RUSTIC STYLE COMES HOME

"Why Not a Wigwam Style?" asked one article in an 1895 issue of *The Decorator and Furnisher,* whose pages often showcased model rooms complete with imitation-log wall coverings, horn-legged stools, stuffed owls, and a few tomahawks or canoe paddles thrown in for good measure. Other magazines of the period answered the growing mania for twig chairs, antler light fixtures, and rawhide lamp shades with their own regular features on rustic decorating.

In an era that prized romance and exoticism, it was only a matter of time before hunting spears became curtain rods and snowshoes replaced the traditional ancestral portrait over the mantel. This, after all, was the height of the Victorian age, when clutter was equated with good taste and cultural breadth. Talismans from the untamed wilderness were welcome additions to the ever-expanding mix and helped create a decorating style free of European influence. Mostly, however, birch-bark picture frames, Indian trade blankets, and twigwork porch brackets appealed for precisely the same reasons as they do today: they surprise and delight, reflect the value of natural materials and handcraftsmanship, and establish a sense of history and place.

The rustic style is unquestionably, quintessentially American. A truly democratic melting pot of decorating and design, the look encompasses with equal ease the plain Craftsman oak of Gustav Stickley from the early 1900s and the cowboy furniture of Thomas Molesworth from several decades later. Rustic rooms work by instinct, appealing to our national passion for collecting and relying on the power of association and emotion to draw us in. Displayed to advantage, everyday objects—a piece of Hopi pottery, antique fishing creels—become works of art as well as important links to roots and memories.

Not surprisingly, the taste for rustic design is stronger than ever. While vintage cowboy art, western furniture, and North Woods pieces intricately crafted from twigs and bark are in high demand, regional artists and artisans have also adopted the style. Their charming accessories and furniture for house and garden evoke the spirit of the wilderness and make the warm, down-home look of rustic accessible to everyone.

Requisite decoration for early camps, birch-bark accessories suited the Victorian taste for eclecticism but remain remarkably undated today. Picture frames at Bircholm hold early photographs of this turn-of-the-century camp on Upper Saranac Lake in the Adirondacks.

THE GREAT OUTDOORS

Setting means everything. A new cabin incorporates glass walls to bring in mountain views (left). The owners of a Montana ranch encompassing more than ten thousand acres (above) have added paths and bridges to enhance enjoyment of the scenery. In the picturesque tradition, a bench offers a pausing point.

PORCHES AND TERRACES

In a wilderness retreat, porches are extra rooms
that stretch the seasons. A fireplace takes the chill
off the night air on the screened porch of a New
England lake house (opposite). Rope railings enclose
the deck of a marshland hunting lodge (above), and
a stone-paved terrace becomes an outdoor living
room for a cabin on Woods Bay in Montana (right).

RUSTIC WORK

Taking advantage of what nature offers is an essential part of the rustic conceit.
In an Illinois cabin, timbers were handcrafted to follow the character of the spruce
logs (above), leaving a natural perch for a tiny bird. For a canopy of branches in
a billiards room (right), Daniel Mack, who specializes in rustic craftsmanship, harvested a grove of red cedar trees naturally bent from growing on a windblown hill.

STAIRS

Built from twigs, logs, and bark-covered limbs,
rustic stairs seem to reach naturally for the tree-
tops. Branches curve around a root-bound newel
post in the staircase of a new Montana ranch house
designed by Candace Tillotson-Miller (opposite).
To make elegant treads in a Montana house, cedar
half logs (above) were stripped of bark by hand,
revealing the wood's dark inner core. Peeled and
dried for a year, an antique apple tree had the
right chunkiness for a newel post crafted by Daniel
Mack (right), who let a low-growing branch become
the natural banister. The maple fork balusters are
the trademark of this contemporary craftsman.

FIREPLACES

Stone establishes a strong sense of substance and scale both indoors and out. Natural color runs through the river rock used for a new Montana porch fireplace by Jeff Balch (left). Granite boulders forming the chimney and hearth of a modern Adirondack lodge by Peter Bohlin (above) have an almost primeval beauty.

FURNISHINGS

Hickory furnishings were a staple of early park hotels and woodland camps. In a Montana dining room designed by Lori O'Kane (opposite), the classic chair design has herringbone caning. The twelve-foot-long trestle table of pine planks and the antler chandelier with a rawhide belly were designed for the space. Slender hickory branches lighted with tiny bulbs make an ethereal chandelier for a New Hampshire boathouse (above). A birch-covered dish dresser (right) recalls rustic Adirondack designs.

Beds made from bark-covered sweetgum fill the loft bedroom of an Ozark cabin on Table Rock Lake in Arkansas (opposite). Fish plaques adorn the headboards; vintage flat-reed creels and a cowhide backpack hang on the footboards. Purposely left in place, sprouting sticks and twigs become hat and clothes pegs. A Pennsylvania cabin (above) displays an Indian shirt, a birch basket, and a leather yoke.

WILD AND WOOLLY

Wildlife can come indoors with clever brushwork,
such as the bear murals on the bathroom walls
(left) and door (above) designed by Allen Ransome
for a retreat in upstate New York. At a Montana
ranch (opposite), a painted deer keeps watch over
an old schoolhouse desk where the owner ties
fishing flies. The furniture recalls the history
of this fishing cabin, which began life as a school
and was moved for its new incarnation.

COWBOYS AND INDIANS

In a Montana lodge from 1917, wool rugs of Navajo and Sorona ancestry underscore the western look (opposite). Lodges of the era often incorporated fireplace inglenooks such as this. A lodgepole pine desk and lamp in the bedroom of a former 1920s dude ranch, also in Montana (above), recall the rugged cowboy designs of Thomas Molesworth, a noted Wyoming furniture maker.

CALL OF THE WILD

EARLY CAMPS AND CABINS

The frenzy for "roughing it" in the wilds took Americans deep into some of the country's most remote areas, where beginning in the 1870s they built thousands of private getaways ranging from one-room mountain cabins to compounds of four thousand acres. Although many city dwellers lived in unimaginable luxury by the end of the century, people still wanted to get away from it all.

The call of the wild led anywhere there were dramatic views, pure mountain air, and unspoiled waterways: the Adirondacks, the Great Lakes, and, by the early 1900s, the West. The last frontier had become irresistible, partly because of romantic cowboy novels and the fabulous success of William Cody's Wild West Show. During World War I the western dude ranch vacation became popular because Europe was off limits. Some dude ranches took after the Great Camps: a main lodge, separate bedroom cabins, stables, storehouses, a saddlery, barns, and ice houses. Many dudes returned to build ranches of their own—typically in an easterner's image of the wild West.

These and other retreats were often eccentric overstatements of woodland conceit, papered with birch bark, chock full of antlers and stuffed squirrels, and so oversized that

the staff necessary to keep them running generally out-numbered the household. Other homes in the wilds were simple affairs offering the spiritual communion that such nature-minded writers as Ralph Waldo Emerson espoused. But whether large or small, the best cabins, lodges, camps, and ranches combined rustic furnishings and a rough-hewn architecture of wood and stone complete with porches, walkways, and open-air rooms to encourage outdoor living. A deliberately inaccessible site might take hours or even days to reach, but that was precisely the point: once visitors finally got there, they felt privileged to be in the middle of nowhere.

Deep emotional attachments have bound owners to their historic vacation homes, and many have stayed in the same families for generations. But even new owners who are restoring them in increasing numbers recognize that America's early camps and cabins offer an invaluable opportunity for solitude and escape while they encap-sulate the history of the wilderness experience itself.

Although he had no formal architectural training, Benjamin Muncil, the Adirondack craftsman who built Camp Topridge's boathouse in the 1920s, had a superb eye for the natural forms of branches and vines.

MILLIONAIRES' PLAYGROUND

More than a century has passed since work began on Sagamore Lodge, but anyone who journeys down the entrance drive cannot fail to be stirred by the same distant beauty that lured William West Durant to this wilderness site in the heart of New York's Adirondack lake country. Durant, a real estate developer and self-taught architect who is considered the father of the Great Camp, began Sagamore in 1896. The ensemble of log and bark-papered buildings on Shedd Lake epitomized the concept of a multipurpose, multibuilding retreat for "roughing it" with the aid of every comfort, including radiator heat, gas lighting, and hot and cold running water. Sagamore was a gentleman's estate, conceived as a working farm. Durant's third major camp, it would prove his greatest triumph and his greatest folly, costing a quarter of a million dollars and finally driving him into bankruptcy.

Like most woodland camps of its type, Sagamore was a continual work in progress. One of Durant's chief contributions was the chalet-style main lodge (page 19), a massive three-story structure housing a central sitting room, five bedrooms, dressing rooms, and a study. Among the hodgepodge of furnishings were wicker, folding canvas camp chairs, Indian-pattern throw rugs, animal skins, and hunting trophies.

Faced with mounting debt, Durant sold the camp, lake, and fifteen hundred acres in 1901 to Alfred G. Vanderbilt, whose own improvements included electricity, telephones, an underground sewage system, a bowling alley, and a billiards hall. After his death aboard the *Lusitania* in 1915, his widow, Margaret, continued the camp expansion, adding private bedroom cabins and enlarging the dining room to accommodate seventy-five. Winter visitors, met at the train station with horse-drawn sleighs, were wrapped in ermine robes for the ride back to camp, where they were greeted with a display of Roman candles. Sagamore, nicknamed the "playground of the millionaires," eventually counted ninety-nine bedrooms and twenty-three baths.

Sagamore's main lodge and adjacent kitchen–dining room structure formed the core of the family compound, set well apart from the farm and service buildings. The camp is now used by a conservation group for environmental programs.

A roof-covered dock (above) fronts the former
Shedd Lake, which Durant renamed Sagamore
Lake after a character from the popular novel
The Last of the Mohicans. By the early 1900s
bowling had become all the rage. Six-foot-deep
concrete footings kept the floor of the Vanderbilts'
two-lane, open-air alley (right) from warping.

ADIRONDACK HIGH

By the 1920s extravagant entertaining in the wilds had become such an important part of the Gilded Age social calendar that Emily Post's *Etiquette* dedicated an entire chapter to the Adirondack house party. The book highly recommended pampering visitors, lest roughing it in the woods too closely resemble the real thing. No concern at Camp Topridge: each private guest cottage featured a sitting room, fireplace, bar, and panel of call bells to summon a private hairdresser or fishing guide. Among the splendidly improbable diversions were first-run movie screenings, floating dinner parties, and square dances held in a log replica of a Russian *dacha*.

Topridge today remains one of the great wilderness retreats of the Adirondack Mountains. An essay in rustic evolution, the recently refurbished compound of more than fifty timber-and-stone buildings began as a modest late-nineteenth-century lodge called Kanosa. In the early 1920s, the cereal heiress Marjorie Merriweather Post purchased the camp and redesigned it according to plans by Benjamin Muncil, a local builder, to incorporate dozens of cabins, lodges, and service buildings strung along an eighty-foot-high hogback ridge. Visitors to the waterlocked complex, originally accessible only by boat, were greeted at the spectacular boathouse embellished with bark-covered cedar and then carried by open-air funicular to the ridgetop main lodge, where an Eskimo kayak, antelope chandeliers, and Geronimo's war bonnet completed the decor.

Intimate seating areas incorporating some original furnishings from the Marjorie Merriweather Post era help break up the 2,500-square-foot living room of the main lodge. Among the new rustic pieces designed for the space is a center table with antler-entwined legs by the Adirondack craftsman Barney Bellinger.

The recent renovation has rescued the camp from two decades of neglect and reflects the present owners' desire to create a private family compound for entertaining in the spirit of the Great Camps of old. In the same tradition, the three-year project relied on a multidisciplinary team of artists, craftspeople, architects, designers, and local builders. The original boathouse, funicular, *dacha*, and lodge have been restored, and several new guest cabins, largely the work of the lead architect Richard Giegengack, are tucked into the one-hundred-acre site in a villagelike grouping.

The latest designs reveal the strong influence of northern European folk architecture, but they also have the rustic soul of local Adirondack buildings. In each, the interior designer Nancy Rogers of Rogers-Ford used paintings and objects from the owners' collection, adding textured fabrics and new pieces. At the same time Adirondack furnishings from the Post era keep the camp's history alive. The overall design is notable for its attention to detail, evident in intricate twig tambour work, inlays of rare woods, and woodland nature carvings that pay homage to the high level of craftsmanship fundamental to the Great Camp tradition.

Post originally named her retreat Hutridge after her second husband, E. F. Hutton. Among their first additions was the boathouse, where tree-trunk supports appear to grow from the floor. The collection of vintage vessels includes Adirondack lake boats.

The boathouse (left) was intended as a spectacular first sight for visitors arriving by water. The new cabin next to it is called Lothrop's after the camp's original nineteenth-century owners. As in Post's day, each guest room at Topridge has a theme; Lothrop's (above) was inspired by Norwegian folk art.

PLAIN LIVING

New York's Adirondack Mountains, it has been said, are where easterners first learned to love the wilds. Putnam Camp is where the affair continues. This ensemble of wood buildings spilling down a hillside meadow in Keene Valley is one of the oldest Adirondack summer retreats and among the least changed. The original farmhouse and rustic cabins are maintained, along with such well-entrenched customs as sunrise climbs and music in the open-air parlor known as the Stoop. Such hard tradition is the real fabric of the early Adirondack camps, which were built as much on sentiment, memory, and improvisation as on foundations of timber and stone.

Putnam Camp's origins reflect Keene Valley's own history as the nineteenth-century haunt of poets, writers, and landscape painters, including Winslow Homer, Asher Durand, and Thomas Cole. In 1877 four friends from Boston acquired the house and outbuildings of the old Beede farm, then a simple boarding house used by many of the visitors who came to "tramp" up Adirondack peaks with ominously accurate names such as Wolf's Jaw, Gothics, and Sawtooth.

The new owners were the Harvard philosopher William James, Henry P. Bowditch, James Putnam, and his brother, Charles Putnam, all like-minded intellectuals who believed in "plain living and high thinking." Each summer their camp filled with Harvard faculty and other colleagues (including Carl Jung and a reluctant Sigmund Freud), lured to the valley for a sample of woodland salon culture. Although accommodations were spartan, the plain living was "liberal and of the best."

The camp itself is a place of odds and ends, evolving piecemeal in the manner of many Adirondack retreats. In the first year, a one-and-one-half-story bedroom shanty was built. More sleeping cabins for friends and family members followed, including one christened the Ark during a three-day downpour in 1905. The old barn was converted into a workshop and produced furniture as needed. The last cabin was added in 1916. Except for the addition of electricity and plumbing, there have been few changes since, and Putnam Camp continues to offer an unspoiled patch of wilderness living.

"Never let me forget it is perfect here," pleaded a family member of early days at Putnam Camp. A new bridge (above) maintains the rustic tradition. Tourists to Keene Valley increased so rapidly in the 1870s that Smith Beede opened a hotel after selling his house to the Putnams. The old farmhouse (opposite) contains the private camp's dining room.

During his 1909 visit, Sigmund Freud wrote home that breakfast was "very original and plentiful." An egg-and-dart motif painted during the nineteenth century (above) still decorates the dining room where Freud enjoyed his meals. Even the table arrangement (right) remains as it was in Putnam Camp's early days.

BEYOND THE BIRCHES

Sin-ha-lo-nen-ne-pus, the Indian name for Upper Saranac Lake in New York state, means "large and beautiful lake" or "lake of the beautiful sky." Either translation is appropriate because Upper Saranac is a quintessential Adirondack landscape of water, mountain, and sky. As early as 1850, hunters and other visitors began stopping here at an inn called the Rustic Lodge, and by 1900 as many as fifty private camps had sprung up. Today the thirty-seven-mile shoreline is protected under the "forever wild" provision of New York's 1894 constitution.

The picturesque collection of wood buildings now known as Bircholm was begun on a wooded island around 1887 and remains in the same family that purchased it from the original owners in 1916. Unpretentious but elegantly composed, the compound includes five shingled cottages and three boathouses linked by trim pine-needle paths and a woodland color scheme in dark green and brown. Bircholm is smaller in scale than the fabulous rustic palaces of Adolph Lewisohn (Prospect Point), Governor Levi P. Morton (Pinebrook), Otto Kahn (Bull Point), and Isaac Seligman (Sekon) that made the southern end of the lake a celebrated turn-of-the-century retreat for the Jewish gentry, but it follows a similar pattern.

Most of Bircholm's carefully sited buildings stand close to the lake, although groves of conifers and birches mask them to preserve privacy. Its covered runway connecting the dining building to the main cottage is also a classic Great Camp feature, a descendant of early Adirondack tent-platform camps in which separate tents joined by boardwalks served separate uses.

Bircholm's distinct sense of design is evident in the chalet-style features of the main boathouse and in beautiful Craftsman-period wainscoting found throughout the interiors. Carefully placed verandas, picture windows, and projecting dormers also help establish the congenial conversation between structure and nature that was the hallmark of good camp planning. The peeled-pole porch brackets and railings are charming if predictable exterior details, but the refined use of woodland materials inside is an imaginative nod to the decorative talents of nature itself.

Bircholm is still owned by descendants of Edmund and Carolyn Lyon, who bought it in 1916. A built-in bench outside the dining room (above) is a fitting allusion to the camp's original name, Rest-a-While. The main cottage (opposite) gained a full second story in 1913, when the rustic gable decoration was added.

The whole point of the Adirondack camp was outdoor living, and Bircholm's broad veranda (left) still functions as an open-air living room. As at other retreats, a covered boardwalk (above) connects the main cottage to a separate building housing a dining room, kitchen, and former servants' sitting room.

In addition to being fashionable, birch-bark wall coverings helped lighten
the dark interiors of early Adirondack camps. The gridded wood-spat design
in the entry hall of Bircholm's main cottage (above) is particularly sophisticated.
In the camp's dining room (right), shingles create a more rustic finish.

BOATHOUSE ABODE

Using changing levels and natural materials, the architect Augustus Shepard carefully integrated his camps to their sites and opened up the interiors with picture windows and dormers. The covered walkway to the left of the boathouse (opposite) leads up the hill to a separate bedroom structure. Inspired by Victorian designs, a thronelike chair made by Jerry Farrell (above) was fashioned from rhododendron roots, a traditional material in early rustic furniture.

Tucked into a hillside on Little Moose Lake near Old Forge, New York, this beautifully sited boathouse came from the hand of Augustus D. Shepard, one of the relatively few Adirondack camp designers whose work is well documented. It is a trademark Shepard design known as the boathouse camp, which the architect devised specifically for steep lakeside sites. The shingled structure, restored by Barbara and Thad Collum, doubles as the camp's main lodge, enclosing a boat room at water level, with the sitting room, dining room, and kitchen situated directly above. The bedrooms occupy a separate building, linked to the boathouse by a covered walkway. An integral part of the tightly conceived layout is its enclosed garden patio, another Shepard characteristic, which forms a protected outdoor living room.

Shepard had close family ties to the Adirondacks and was said to have had an "early and zealous affection for their rough wild beauty." His eye for balance, light, and structural elegance is perhaps nowhere more apparent than in this camp, designed for George Storm, a dealer in rare woods, in 1924.

On the primary, lakeside facade, twin octagonal towers with candle-snuffer roofs evoke the charm of Victorian resort architecture. Inside, ample proportions and a hipped ceiling give the central sitting room a distinct sense of openness. To enhance that effect, the room is shaped as a perfect twenty-eight-foot square and pared down to its bare studs and log roof purlins, so that its simple geometric beauty becomes the main focus of the design. Because windows and views frame the room on all four sides, light continually reflects off the water and plays into different corners, picking up the warm tones of the heart pine floor as morning folds into afternoon.

A geometric pattern of trusses and rafters deliberately draws the eye up to the living room's open ceiling (left top). The rare rustic cellarette next to the dining alcove (left bottom) was designed by Shepard. A collection of antique miniatures (above) includes doll chairs and furniture sales samples. The angled profile of the towers accommodates additional windows to maximize light, making the second alcove off the living room (opposite) a bright sitting area. The architect customarily oversaw details such as the boathouse's iron hardware and cast-iron wall fixtures, which are original.

The designer Barbara Collum revived the original camp wicker with dark green paint (opposite), refinished the sofa table, which was discovered in a workshed, and added a vegetable dye rug.

In the master bedroom (above), a young tree appears to grow from the headboard of an ironwood bed crafted by the Indian Lake artisan Ken Heitz, while the footboard incorporates a bench.

JOLLY CAMP

A boardwalk bridge connects the small shanty (opposite) with a second, larger cabin. Lapping the shore just inches from the kitchen window (above), water surrounds the island camp, where a restoration has carefully preserved the rustic flavor.

According to an old New Hampshire saying, Lake Winnipesaukee claims an island for every day of the year. Scarcely large enough to be counted are two cabin-sized rock piles, strung together by a boardwalk bridge. The equally diminutive red-shingle buildings on them date from around the 1880s, making the camp one of the oldest survivors in New Hampshire's lake region.

Known locally as the Harvard Islands, this corner of rustic solitude is located off Winnipesaukee's northern shore near Center Harbor. Even before the town became an important steamboat port in the 1850s, it served as an overnight stop on the Boston-Conway stage line bringing travelers into the White Mountain wilderness. As early as 1839 the area was cited by the *New Hampshire Gazetteer* for "the unrivalled beauty of the scenery" and became the lake's first tourist destination. With the railroad era came more visitors, and the region continued to prosper as a fashionable summer resort between the Civil War and World War I, when it supported dozens of boarding houses, hotels, and lakeside camps.

Nineteenth-century photographs identify the two wood-frame buildings on the Harvard Islands as the Jolly Camp, which appears to have been a year-round stopover for anglers, duck hunters, ice skaters, and picnickers. The smaller cabin is a single-room shanty occupied by an enormous corner fireplace, the other a larger structure of one-and-one-half-stories with a lean-to kitchen, a fireplace, two bedrooms, and a winding staircase with a birch banister.

Sometime before 1914 both cabins gained verandas supported on posts made from tree limbs. Not much else has changed, but that is just the idea. For the family that spends summer weekends here today, the simple life is the best life. The camp, restored by the architect Christopher Williams, is still without plumbing or electricity and remains the refuge from civilization it was always intended to be.

As early as 1839 New Hampshire's Center Harbor region was hailed by the *New England Gazetteer* as "a delightful resting spot," and it still is. Lake Winnipesaukee (left) takes its name from an apt Indian word meaning "smile of the god." At the main cabin on Harvard Islands (above), a lakeside tree becomes a natural part of the design, shading a second-story deck that opens off the upstairs bedroom.

In the small living room of the main cabin (above), birch saplings form a rustic banister for stairs leading to the upstairs bedroom. The stone fireplace is original. Kerosene lanterns and candlesticks with whimsical bark shades (opposite) provide light for the camp, which has never been electrified. Little has changed within the wood-frame structure since it was built in the late nineteenth century.

AN ARK RUN AGROUND

New Hampshire architecture displays the same characteristics often used to describe the people of this hard-bitten New England state: solid, independent, and stubbornly idiosyncratic. High Haith Lodge on Squam Lake is a bit of all three. Named for a nearby sheep meadow (*haith* in Scottish), the house is part of an island summer colony that grew up in the early 1900s, drawing families from Boston, Philadelphia, and New York.

Its ample proportions and rambling floor plan are holdovers from the late Victorian period, but the original eccentric composition of eyebrows, overhangs, and sleeping porches gives the retreat a strong personality all its own. Situated just a few yards from the water, the shingled structure—organized around a two-story hexagonal atrium finished with shiplap pine—resembles nothing so much as an ark run aground. It is everything a summer house should be.

High Haith Lodge was designed around 1906 for a Brookline, Massachusetts, family by Joseph Randolph Coolidge II, a Boston architect whose own family spent summers on Squam near the village of Sandwich. Because there was as yet no road to the property, the materials had to be skidded across the ice from the steamboat dock at Ashland after the lake froze over in winter. The lodge changed hands during World War II, remained virtually unaltered for the next half century, and was recently refurbished by new owners.

Although Joseph Randolph Coolidge received his formal architectural training at the École des Beaux-Arts in Paris in the 1890s, his design for High Haith Lodge has a strong vernacular feel that gives it enormous character. The asymmetrical roofline and dark exterior blend the rambling summer house naturally into the surrounding forest, while informal landscaping accentuates the naturalistic effect.

The renovation, by the New Hampshire architect Christopher Williams and the interior designer Carole Bailey, quietly emphasizes comfort while preserving the original structural design, which Coolidge had purposely distilled to its elements, leaving studs, joists, and brackets exposed. Reinforced and rewired, the lodge gained a remodeled kitchen and new master bathroom, installed in a former second-story sleeping porch. Unobtrusive lighting brightens the dark interior and picks out the profiles of brackets and railings from the shadows, playing up the structural geometry.

From spring to autumn, three walls stay open to make the atrium and adjoining dining room one with a rambling screened porch. This close connection with the outdoors reflects Coolidge's own familiarity with the vicissitudes of the lake's climate: deep roof overhangs shade the interior from sun and shelter it from the squalls that roll across Squam on summer evenings.

On the porch, a clever pulley system allows entire wall sections to open and close easily (below). Using the unusual octagonal floor plan to advantage, the designer Carole Bailey assembled a symmetrical furniture grouping in the atrium living room (right), where new wicker chairs are grounded on a circular rug. The original shiplap novelty siding was rubbed with oil to bring out its color.

Hanging from an adjustable chain, the original
camp lantern (opposite) has been electrified but
still casts a gentle light. Interior windows, opening
onto a remodeled sleeping porch, and exposed
joists (above) underscore an informal, camplike
atmosphere. Despite a major overhaul, the rustic
look is also preserved in the remodeled kitchen
(right), where a new china cabinet is fitted with
chicken-wire doors. A master bath now occupies
the former sleeping porch (page 84). In the guest
room (page 85), a Victorian bed holds its own.

SOUTHERN SADDLEBAG

A step back not in time but in memory—that is the effect of Logan Hill Lodge, a rustic bed-and-breakfast that evokes the pioneer spirit of rural Kentucky. Many visitors grew up in or near this tiny hamlet of Gravel Switch, as did their ancestors. So when they step inside the door of the old log building furnished with patchwork quilts, washtubs, wood-burning stoves, and other mementos of local life from generations past, they immediately connect. "A lot of them are seeing things they haven't laid eyes on since they were children," says owner Ed Lanham. "People will start to reminisce, and it's wonderful to sit and listen to them."

Lanham created his appealing lodge by moving two abandoned eighteenth-century cabins to the seven-hundred-acre farm where he raises spotted Jacob sheep and shelters orphaned deer. He discovered the first cabin by accident, hidden deep in the fields, its squared beech timbers covered by weatherboard. Reconstructed in its new spot, this classic southern "saddlebag"—two rooms flanking a central breezeway—forms the main section of the house. A second cabin, built in 1785 of hewn oak logs, became a rear wing. In a painstaking restoration process, Lanham carefully dismantled the timbers and beams of both buildings piece by piece, numbered them, and then rebuilt them with a mud-colored chinking to set off the weathered-gray wood. Doors were stripped and reused, and the original masonry was saved. Some thirteen thousand new shakes hand split from red oak cover the roof.

These aged log structures are imbued with history and meaning, Lanham is convinced. Inside, the air of authenticity is reinforced by beams and joists left exposed and furnishings with personal connections. As he built and furnished the house, Lanham went day by day, with no formal plan. "However it turned out was the way it was going to be," he says. "I just let it happen. If it had been better planned, it probably wouldn't have worked nearly as well."

Weathered to a soft gray, beech timbers dating from the 1700s are well preserved (above). Willow furniture graces a new porch, which replaced the dilapidated original. Occupying the larger saddlebag cabin, the living room (opposite) has handmade furnishings such as a bent hickory rocker and a matching swing crafted by local Amish artisans. The chandelier was fashioned from antlers shed by one of the farm's whitetail deer. The poplar floor is new.

Still used, the woodburning cookstove (left) once belonged to Lanham's grandmother. The oak butcher block is the work of an elderly neighbor. In the dining area (above), country table settings await visitors who can navigate down the ladderlike staircase, taken from the smaller cabin, which dates to 1785.

DAM SITE BETTER

An insatiable salvager who runs an antiques shop, Cynthia Dupps talked a bait store owner out of his sign to make a bench for her living room (opposite). Typical of her finds, an antique cabinet from Oklahoma displays fishing gear and turkey calls (above).

When the owners of this rustic retreat in Arkansas began using it on weekends several years ago, it was just far enough away from their Dentonville home "to feel like another part of the world." Dating from the late 1920s or early 1930s, the log cabin below Beaver Lake Dam in the White River region stands five hundred yards from the water's edge on a fifteen-hundred-acre wilderness tract that is home to an extraordinary range of Ozark wildlife, including deer, coyotes, bobcats, turkeys, fox, quail, roadrunners, white bass, blue herons, and spoonbills.

The four-room cabin, dubbed Dam Site Better, was resurrected from a state of serious disrepair and turned into a cozy lodge by Cynthia and Kirk Dupps, avid collectors of country wares who share an affinity for the comfortable, rough-hewn spirit of log buildings. The old retreat, originally used for fishing and hunting, was built of cedar logs harvested on the property and consisted of two rooms and a screened porch added in 1941. There were few amenities other than a spring-fed, gravity-operated water system and two fireplaces, including one on the porch, which the family still uses.

The cabin had been abandoned for years and was in rough shape, minus its windows and doors. Although the old hogs'-hair mortar needed some rechinking, the heartwood cedar logs—rock hard and water resistant—were in excellent condition. The couple enclosed the porch to create a small bedroom, bunkroom, and bath but took pains to preserve the building's homely character. Stripping the heartwood pine floors of three layers of paint, the owners purposely left random patches of the old finish for a bit of unexpected texture. A fresh color scheme of red and green adds contemporary charm, while the surprising glossy finish on cabinetry, doors, and ceilings helps throw light back into the rooms to brighten an otherwise dim interior.

This cheerful decor is complemented by eclectic furnishings and accessories arranged for informal comfort. Wingback chairs mix easily with nineteenth-century scrubbed pine from New England, hunting memorabilia, rustic Ozark pieces fashioned from hickory, primitive garden tools, and fishing tackle. This accumulation represents more than three decades of hunting and "picking" for antiques by the Duppses, whose astute eye for the unusual has resulted in an unmistakable atmosphere of friendly welcome. "Log cabins seem to embrace you," says Kirk Dupps.

One of the few concessions to convenience is a bathroom (above). Interior shutters were added here and throughout the cabin for security and privacy. The cabin is just yards from the water, so fishing poles are kept handy. When not in use, they become part of the decor (opposite).

The high-gloss paint finish used on the ceiling helps throw more light into the kitchen (opposite). The Duppses shop for furniture at local flea markets but also travel as far as New England to pick up scrubbed pine. An unusual find, the vintage painting over the dining table (above) is one of a dozen commissioned by the George T. Stagg Brewing Company for loan to its best customers.

REGULAR DUDES

Lonesome Land is an apt description for Wyoming, where there are three cows for every person. The landscape and the cowboy myth are larger than life here, and Wyoming hospitality is also something of a legend. The state has been the center of dude ranching since the custom of taking in paying guests for a taste of the West began in earnest around World War I.

Recently restored and refurnished, this former dude ranch on the North Fork of the Shoshone River occupies the site of a pioneer homestead about thirty miles from Cody. The ranch was started as the Circle H in 1926 to host pack trips for young men from eastern military academies into Yellowstone Park and Shoshone National Forest and over the Continental Divide. Early accommodations consisted of "tepee tents," but by 1930 the Circle H was welcoming regular dudes, and the owners (local ranchers who raised Hereford cattle) replaced the tents with log guest cabins they built by hand.

The six guest cabins and the main lodge proved ideal in spirit and size for the current owners, a large family attracted by the privacy of the property, adjacent to the Shoshone wilderness. Refurbished by the architect Jonathan Foote, the log structures have been rechinked, wired for electricity, and scrubbed clean of soot accumulated from kerosene lanterns. The main lodge now contains a sitting room, dining room, kitchen, and bedroom suite, while each cabin includes a bedroom, bath, and porch shaded by the roof's projecting eaves.

A new interior design blends an existing collection of western artwork with dozens of new furnishings rich in cowboy spirit, the work of the Cody designers Virginia and J. Mike Patrick, Wyoming natives who credit their inspiration to the noted cowboy furniture maker and craftsman Thomas Molesworth. Their handcraftsmanship and detailing underscore a western theme that combines the rugged mentality of a cattle wrangler with the comfort and familiarity of a well-worn saddle.

Log cabins at the former Circle H, now known as Star Hill Ranch, have been carefully rehabilitated to serve as guest cottages (above and opposite). A private family retreat, the Wyoming compound began as a dude ranch in the 1920s. The term *dude* was first coined in Yellowstone Park in 1886; *dudine* referred to a woman and *dudette* to a child.

Distinguished by witty detail—slash stitching, rope piping, horn handles—
the Patricks' designs lend cowboy spirit to the living room (left) and dining room
(above), where chair seats are covered in Navajo blankets. Lodgepole pine pieces
from their Cody studio, New West, include a "cloud" bed (page 100) and (page 101,
clockwise from top left) a rolling bar upholstered in red leather, a relief-carved
chest, and a chunky dresser and dressing table with burl legs and studded tops.

In the rustic Great Room (opposite), cedar tree
trunks by the hearth appear to grow right out
of the floor. To create unusual texture and preserve
the wood, builders shaved off the outer bark of
each log but left the cambium layer intact. Outside,
a stone gallery surrounds a secluded rear court
(above). Large multipane windows and French doors
flood the Great Room with daylight (page 104).
During the early years, local residents stayed on
the payroll throughout the winter, cutting ice and
crafting furniture such as a rustic bench (page 105).

Kootenai Lodge, built on the site of a long-vanished
Kootenai Indian encampment, is a fascinating portrait of
how the rustic tradition traveled west. With its log-and-
stone lodges, guest cabins, and farm buildings edging the
shore of Swan Lake near Big Fork, Montana, this historic summer
compound has all the elements of the classic Great Camp: unspoiled
scenery, an ambitious scale, and a rugged design that reveals the
unified hand of a professional architect and a local builder. The log
buildings at Kootenai Lodge are notable for their fine workmanship,
highlighted by perfect saddle-notched corner joints. Copper and slate,
tamarack and cedar, all help make a particularly sensitive transition
from building to landscape.

A few of the cabins may date to as early as 1901, when a homesteader
named Zadok Johnston received a land patent here for 127 acres. In
1908 the property was sold to Orvis Evans and Cornelius ("Con") Kelley, attorneys who would later become chief counsel and president,
respectively, of the Anaconda Copper Mining Company. Evans and
Kelley envisioned a summer estate for their families, but Kootenai soon
expanded into a $2 million vacation retreat for the mining company's
New York associates. In its glory days during the 1920s, the 2,700-acre
compound encompassed sleeping cabins, a dining room and bar, a
lodge, an office, a billiards hall, a tennis court, and an extensive service complex including a private laundry, a twenty-one-stall barn, and
a five-bay garage with a special platform for washing cars.

The main lodge, built in 1921, is attributed to Kirkland Cutter, a Spokane,
Washington, architect who had designed Lucy Carnegie's 1902 Adirondack camp and the 1914 Lake McDonald Lodge in Montana's Glacier
National Park. For Kootenai's fourteen-thousand-square-foot lodge,
Cutter used an innovative U-shaped plan, placing two rear wings of
guest rooms hacienda-style around an inner courtyard to maximize
sunlight and summer breezes.

ROARING TWENTIES RUSTIC

A triumph of rusticity, the Chief Joseph Ranch was well suited to its remote Montana location. Log trusses add drama to the Great Room (opposite), while local river rock creates an imposing entry (above). The current owners have restored William Ford's 1920 Montana getaway, where they now raise pureblooded horses and champion bulls.

Legend has it that guests invited to the party celebrating the completion of William Ford's log-and-stone lodge near Montana's Bitterroot Mountains in 1920 arrived at the Darby train station in nine private railroad cars. It was a housewarming that suited the house. An essay in extravagance typical of its pre-income-tax day, the five-thousand-square-foot structure required $50,000, three years to build, and two dozen workers to harvest the sixty-foot lodgepole pine timbers. The house had five bedrooms, electrified light fixtures from Tiffany and Company, and hardware fittings of solid brass.

A prominent Ohio glass tycoon, Ford acquired fifteen hundred acres of forest and pasture in the Bitterroot Valley near the Idaho border to bail his son out of a real estate venture gone bad in 1915. In the process he fell in love with the land, doubled his holdings, and established a prize-winning dairy ranch. The new lodge (named by a later owner after the Nez Percé leader Chief Joseph) was planned as a western country house where Ford and his family could escape from humid Cincinnati summers. It was the first log commission by the Toledo firm of Bates and Gamble, and its European chalet style shows in its steep roofline. The battered stone piers are reminiscent of Robert Reamer's 1903 Old Faithful Inn at Yellowstone National Park.

The design captures the spirit of the wilderness in its use of local materials—timber and river rocks from the ranch's own property—and its exaggerated scale does justice to the majesty of the western landscape. The lodgepole pine logs measure as much as two feet in diameter, and at 2,200 square feet the main living space, a two-story Great Room, takes up almost half of the lodge's entire space. The impressive design was matched by the level of craftsmanship. Each log was hand-fitted to the next, producing a structure that remains completely sound three-quarters of a century after the last log was laid in place.

An enormous entrance hall with a grand staircase was a typical feature of early-twentieth-century country houses. A vintage rolltop desk tucks under the half-log stair risers (above), and original built-in benches frame an inglenook (right). Building the lodge was a labor-intensive project: each log was carried to the site with leather straps to minimize damage and protect the bark.

ROUGHING IT

RUSTIC STYLE REVISITED

A potent symbol of respite and escape, the log cabin has never lost its hold on the American consciousness. Since the pioneer era, this revered national icon has been inseparable from the concepts of honesty, rugged individualism, and frontier spirit. Physically, it embodies a back-to-basics rusticity that connects us to the landscape. Emotionally, it brings us to a place far removed from daily routine, where a campfire and the constellations wheeling across an ink-black sky banish cares, cleanse the soul, and open the imagination to the boundless possibilities for adventure and romance.

Who doesn't long for a piece of the wilderness to call one's own? Almost no one, if the number, geographic range, and stylistic scope of today's new wilderness vacation homes are any measure. "The more society becomes high tech, the more demand there is for rustic design," explains one Montana builder who specializes in traditional log structures. "Here we have the oldest building form in America, and it is more popular than ever. Why? Because it has roots. It gets people back in touch with nature, their family, their friends, and the quality of life ."

These days the term *cabin* is more figurative than literal, and logs are only one option in a range of natural woods and stone with inherent beauty and an ability to forge a relationship between structure and environment. But no matter what the size or type—shanty, camp, lodge, or ranch—the new American retreat expresses a desire for good design that celebrates nature and acknowledges America's remarkable heritage of regional craft and building traditions. It often represents an attempt to capture childhood memories or the spirit of a place held dear. And while fulfilling the desire for quiet and solitude, it must also be a welcoming home that people can fill with friends and family. Even the newest of houses can seem comfortable and well loved, as building and furnishings take on the character of their materials, the forest, and the owners themselves.

Home to a Pennsylvania couple who wished to return to their country roots, this two-story living room is an expansive, light-filled space that combines a modern sensibility with the feel of old post-and-beam barn framing. Windows catch vistas of sky and forest.

SCULPTOR'S SANCTUARY

Above the Great Room, which doubles as a studio for the sculptor A. J. Obara Jr., the upstairs loft serves as an office and extra guest room. The desk (opposite) was crafted from two-hundred-year-old chestnut logs from Glacier National Park as well as barn beams. Obara designed the cast-bronze buffalo skulls and arrow pulls. His collection of textiles includes boldly patterned Navajo rugs colored with natural dyes (above). The log trundle bed sleeps two.

The sculptor A. J. Obara Jr. claims he designed his log studio and guest house on the west branch of Pennsylvania's Brandywine River in Unionville by drawing it on a napkin. "I just sketched it out," he recalls, "and said: 'One day I'm going to build my studio, and this is what it is going to be.'" Added near the 1796 Chester County residence Obara shares with his wife, Jane, it is the definitive expression of a man certain of what he wants.

Obara, a specialist in wildlife bronzes, is also a serious hunter and angler who spends much of his time out West and traveling the world. Filled with treasures collected from far-flung locales and his own powerful sculptures, the two-story studio, close to the main house but still private, serves as a workspace and as a guest house for friends and prospective clients. "I wanted people who are thinking of commissioning a sculpture to live here with my pieces in the way they are going to at home," explains the artist. "But I also wanted them to be welcome. So, above all, it is extremely comfortable."

Obara gravitated to a log structure because the rugged Montana pine seemed to answer the immediate connection he feels with the outdoors. "It's warm, it's rustic, and it takes you to nature," he says without hesitation. A Great Room, loft, and kitchen are situated on one level, with a bathroom and bedroom below. Throughout, Native American garments, textured carvings, and graphically patterned blankets, as well as fishing reels and a tribal Indian ladder, create a spontaneous living museum, the objects lighted to accentuate their materials and sculptural forms.

In his studio as in his art, Obara believes that small focal points are vital elements in drawing the viewer in. He has incorporated bits of petrified wood, fossils, arrowheads, and rocks—ancient talismans that strike a mystical chord—into the building fabric. "To me, detail is everything," says the sculptor. "You look at the picture, and it is the details that make it whole."

Following Obara's designs, local Amish craftsmen built the cabin and most of its appointments, including kitchen cupboards faced with wood scraps (above). It took him two decades to gather the Indian artifacts, saddles, and cowboy hats displayed with his hunting trophies in his studio (opposite). A reflection of his love for the great outdoors, they infuse the cabin with genuine wilderness spirit.

The Obaras' lower-level guest bedroom (opposite) hangs over the river, maximizing the views of water and trees. Its chunky, overscaled four-poster is generous enough to accommodate Paul Bunyan. Among the home's salvaged pieces is the 1886 wood-trimmed bathtub (above), purchased at auction and refurbished with a coat of dark green paint applied at a local autobody shop.

THE COMPLEAT ANGLER

Dawn in the wooded valleys of the western Catskills arrives with cool air and a mist rising over the Beaverkill River, one of the most beautiful trout-fishing spots in New York state. Respect for the river and the wilderness preserve around it have been woven into Marsh Lodge, a house of river rock and hand-peeled red pine placed quietly near the water's edge.

"We look at both the Beaverkill and the house as a gift," says Leslie Marsh, who planned the year-round vacation retreat with her husband, David, a passionate fly fisherman. Designed by the architect Donald Breimhurst, Marsh Lodge makes use of a simple spatial plan: the rectangle. The two-and-one-half-story structure, shouldered into a fairly steep hillside, encloses six thousand square feet. On the main floor an open dining room and a private master bedroom flank the central Great Room, where a corner fireplace wall and a sweeping spiral log staircase opposing it are dramatic elements in the two-story space. A loft contains sleeping quarters, balconies, and storage; the lower level holds two more bedrooms and a game room.

The elegant masonry includes brick, native bluestone, and river rock, gathered from the banks of the Delaware River. The hand-peeled red pine logs were harvested in Michigan, but their substantial size (they average twenty inches in diameter) matches the scale of trees in the surrounding Beaverkill woods. Surfaces of stone and log continue uninterrupted from interior to exterior, so that the house looks as though it has been turned inside out. A flagstone terrace, screened dining porch, covered deck, and sun deck further connect the lodge to the Beaverkill landscape.

The furnishings, including handsome Stickley-style pieces and overstuffed chairs, accent the building's own bare, elemental beauty. The buffalo-check upholstery crisply defines areas of color, part of a refreshing red-and-green design scheme. This combines with fishing memorabilia to create the friendly character of a mountain camp. Comments Leslie Marsh: "What else could work as well? A New York mountain lodge look just seemed right."

A battered stone porch pier (above) recalls a design element common in turn-of-the-century bungalows and lodge architecture. The river rock was also used to create a dramatic chimney wall (opposite). A gas fire burns in one of three outdoor fireplaces that permit the Marshes and their two sons to use several terraces and porches throughout the year.

Corner saddle notches distinguish a porch off the
master bedroom (above). Averaging twenty inches
in diameter, more than 230 hand-peeled pine logs
went into the cabin (right). After each was laid in
place to check size and fit in Michigan, the cabin
was dismantled and trucked log by log to the Catskill
Mountains in New York. To blend into the house's
color palette, cabinets in the kitchen (page 122)
were painted green over red. A tall fireplace of river
rock warms the two-story living room (page 123).

The art glass door (opposite), modeled after the entry of Greene and Greene's 1908 Gamble House in Pasadena, California, was made by a local Montana artisan using traditional bronze leading. The painting above the Craftsman sideboard is by Edgar Payne. Morris-style chairs made by Gustav Stickley in the early 1900s occupy the master bedroom (above).

Emphasis on traditional craftsmanship, honest materials, and functional forms makes the Mission furniture of Gustav Stickley and other American Arts and Crafts designers as popular now as when it was first manufactured at the turn of the century. Among its aficionados are the owners of this two-story house near Bozeman, Montana, built to accommodate their growing collection of Stickley-style antiques. The open floor plan, soaring ceilings, and bold expanses of glass are obviously contemporary, but this unusual home also manages to gently straddle time through its references to the Arts and Crafts period.

An influential design movement affecting home furnishings and architecture during the early 1900s and widely promoted by Stickley in his *Craftsman* magazine, the style achieved its most sophisticated expression in the large California residences of the Pasadena architects Greene and Greene. Mission furnishings (so called because they had a mission, or purpose) reflected the same tenets of unfettered design. With their clean lines and minimal decoration, these solid pieces of oak and leather have a timeless appeal and warmth—a good reason that they work so well in any setting.

One of the owners of this new house comes from a fifth-generation California family and owes his interest in Craftsman-era design and Mission furniture to growing up in that state. "I have strong roots in California, and I began studying the Craftsman design tradition when I still lived there," he says. "The more I got into it, the more I understood how this furniture is based on comfort and integrity. I particularly like the form and function."

Over the years the couple have accumulated seating pieces, tables, and lamps by Stickley and competitors Charles P. Limbert and the Lifetime furniture company, along with paintings by pioneer impressionists and contemporary western artists. To make an appropriate showcase for all, they sought an architectural design that would "tone down the western motif" and strongly emphasize workmanship and material. The log construction harks back to Stickley's own affinity for the material, which he associated with the "simple life." Indeed, the entire house hews to the Craftsman credo of beauty and utility.

Quarter-sawn white oak from the Ohio River Valley was used for the cabinets in the kitchen (above) and for the woodwork in the living room (opposite), where the staircase exhibits the clean, simple lines of the Craftsman prototype. Among the paintings on the mantel are works by Russell Chatham, a contemporary western artist. The chandelier was made from outdoor Arts and Crafts fixtures.

SPANISH DREAMS

To build the terrace fireplace (opposite) and court-yard wall (above), the mason Jack McNamara studied Spanish colonial building forms and then adapted traditional adobe designs by using plaster over concrete block. The interior decor (page 130, clockwise from top left) includes a silhouetted lamp by Peter Fillerup that recalls Thomas Molesworth designs; Crow Indian pipe bags and a cloth shirt; transitional weavings and a graphic Germantown rug; and a steer-horn settee. In the living room (page 131), the built-in bench, stepped adobe wall, and *vigas* (beams) are distinctive Spanish colonial features.

Sure in its earthbound simplicity, the architecture of the Southwest, founded in the centuries-old heritage of Spanish colonization, is compelling even today. Colonial influence is clearly apparent in the interplay of rugged logs and smooth adobe-like plaster in this mountain cabin on the East Fork of Idaho's Big Wood River. The house was designed for former Arizonans who are drawn to southwestern building techniques and interiors and are serious collectors of Native American artifacts and western art. Silhouettes and textures of ancient Anasazi pottery, beaded Indian garments, and woven trade blankets complement the architecture's strong character, becoming final, important strokes of drama that bring the building to life.

Oriented to views of Hyndman Peak, the cabin is surrounded by birches and firs. Lodgepole pine and an asymmetrical roofline of pitched gables blend with the natural mountain backdrop; a terrace, walled in with an adobe fireplace, stretches into sheltering groves of trees to create a private outdoor dining space. The bell-shaped fireplace, known as a *fogón*, is a Spanish colonial building feature, traditionally tucked into a corner with a stepped hearth that served as a bench and a place to rest cooking pots. The *portal* (gallery), with its corbeled brackets and herringbone ceiling pattern of peeled *latias* (saplings), also reflects early Spanish roots. The two-sided gallery frames a lawn in the manner of a hacienda courtyard, functioning as a shady porch in summer and catching the low rays of the sun in wintertime.

In the main living area plastered benches and partial walls define the spaces but also keep the basic floor plan open and flowing, an effect amplified by log rafters soaring to the exposed roof peak. Throughout the interior, log beams, bench backs, white walls, and shallow niches become display spaces for objects highlighting the history and culture of the West and Southwest. Among them are paintings by the noted western artists Maynard Dixon and Olaf Seltzer, along with saddles, moccasins, corn-husk bags, and rodeo scarves—everyday objects elegantly showcased as the works of art they are.

GENTLE BENDS

Their peaks worn soft by the millenniums, the Colorado Mountains have a soulful, secretive beauty that strikes a strong chord of emotion in the people who take refuge in this particular region of the West. John Diamond believes that the same should be true of buildings. "Any house needs mystery and life and must hold a place in the landscape," says the architect.

The ten-bedroom vacation retreat he designed for a family of six on a thirty-thousand-acre working ranch a few hours from Denver undeniably pays heed to the territory around it. The single-story wood frame building is enormous, enclosing fourteen thousand square feet and running the length of a football field. But, skimming low, it never competes. The gentle bends of the nearby river are echoed in the structure's massing; trees provide a screen and the mountains a backdrop. "You find yourself working through the site so that you come upon the house rather than slamming into it," Diamond notes.

The sense of mystery is evident as one passes from the low-slung exterior into the spacious, airy living areas. Suddenly space is transformed. Light funnels in through clerestory windows, beams span rooms nine feet up, and ceilings fly skyward to one- and two-way pitches so that "everything rises up."

A mix of materials, including redwood, fir, and Colorado flagstone and exotic woods such as Brazilian cherry, provides texture and variety from room to room, as do the furnishings. It fell to the interior designer Mariette Himes Gomez to make the house feel intimate and lived-in without looking overdecorated. Chunky furniture suits the scale of the rooms, and her nod to frontier lore—birch canoes, cowboy lamps, a poster of Wild Bill Cody—helps ground the house in history and place. While the furniture includes custom-made pieces, there are also plenty of flea market finds. That way visitors always feel at home, and the design never gets too smart for its own good.

To avoid disturbing existing glades of spruce trees and cottonwoods, the architect John Diamond carefully worked the low-slung Colorado ranch house into its riverside site. Smaller sections containing private family and guest suites break off from a central roof ridge extending in a one-hundred-yard line from east to west.

In the hunting lodge tradition, the owners often entertain large parties of friends. Private and public spaces balance: guest suites are complemented by "communal" sitting rooms. Leather upholstery and a Wild Bill Cody poster allude to the wild West (opposite), while rustic frames add a rugged look to cowboy postcards (above).

Work on this Montana spread of some ten thousand acres was a team effort that involved everything from building new bridges, roads, and fencing to salvaging dilapidated barns and outbuildings. A new log cabin (opposite) was added as the main house, and an old schoolhouse was rescued and relocated to serve as a fishing cabin and office (above).

WAY OUT WEST

Part cowgirl, part architect, Candace Tillotson-Miller creates buildings that seem to lean comfortably back on their boot heels and look as sunburned and relaxed as an old wrangler hanging around the corral. Consider, for example, this family compound on a river in southwestern Montana, designed in close collaboration with the interior designers Charles Gandy and Bill Peace and the building firm Yellowstone Traditions. Although work on the three rustic wood cabins was finished only a few years ago, sensitively handled materials and a careful grafting to site play down their youthfulness. Completing the effect is a simple but elegant decor still comfortable enough to allow the family of six to kick up their spurs and enjoy themselves. "They wanted the rooms to be absolutely welcoming from the very beginning," says Tillotson-Miller, "but not so precious that you can't subject them to Montana living."

The trick was to build two wood cabins from scratch (a main house and a two-bedroom bunkhouse for guests), move and revamp an old square-hewn log schoolhouse as an office and fishing cabin, and furnish all three without making them look self-conscious. Architect and designers took their cues from the property itself, a generations-old cattle and hay ranch worn down by hard use. In a landscape dominated by flat hayfields, the two new buildings are near each other in a stand of cottonwood trees that provide shade and a transition in height. The main house has a log veneer over a stick frame to permit large windows and a more flexible design than true log building would allow, and rooms are kept small for an intimate feeling.

Tillotson-Miller was after a traditional look and picked up the local vernacular of the frontier vocabulary: copper screens, simple fir trim, two-over-two windows, and rough-sawn boards. Whenever possible, materials like the rolled rusted tin lining a bathroom were recycled from some of the dilapidated ranch outbuildings. "We thought hard about what can take wear, age gracefully, and even get better with time," says the architect.

The understated furnishings and details determinedly avoid what Gandy and Peace call a "cowboy cliché." Their surprising color palette is an amalgam of soothing greens, chocolatey browns, and rich ochres drawn from bark, leaves, willows, sagebrush, and stones gathered on the ranch. Burlap draperies filter sunlight, and comfortably worn oriental carpets never look too new. Ever sophisticated, the design stops well short of being cute. "We tried not to force the issue," says Charles Gandy. "In the end, we just want you walk into a room and feel like you should be there."

Living areas at the ranch are centered on hearths. The stone fireplace in the new bunkhouse living room (opposite) was deliberately designed with a small firebox to set a cozy scale. A vintage Craftsman rocker stands in the foreground. Dining occurs inside and out. In the main house (left top), a polished cherry mirror and an English oak table add subtle elegance. In the bunkhouse (left bottom), two-over-two windows on the porch reflect the local building vernacular.

Vertical planks of rough-sawn fir side the bunkhouse (left), where log bunks grow into the ceiling (above). In the master bedroom (page 142), an old iron gate makes a new headboard; above it are vintage photographs depicting Old Faithful. Bathrooms too are partly old, partly new (page 143). For example, an outdoor spigot serves a bucket sink (battered to look old) in the powder room (top right), where flattened, corrugated metal covers the walls. For the fishing cabin (bottom right), an old porcelain sink was salvaged, a tree holds towels and toilet paper, a water trough becomes the base of the shower, and soft chamois skins serve as curtains.

UNDER THE BIG SKY

In the Gallatin Valley, where the views earn Montana its reputation as the land of the Big Sky, site and proportion are crucial to good architecture. Both are well integrated in this house of lodgepole pine, larch, and rain-buffed river rock, designed for an East Coast client who wanted a comfortable retreat with a western sensibility. Set gently but firmly in a canyon at the edge of a sage-covered meadow, the low-slung cabin reaches out to grab the landscape. Broad roof planes and log purlins stretching beyond the eaves draw the eye outward, while low stone retaining walls further link the building to the terrain.

Inside, a rugged opulence takes over from the exterior's handsome, unobtrusive presence. With deft emphasis on craftsmanship and materials, the architect, Jerry Locati, has pared the building down to its primitive bones, creating a bold design able to hold its own against the dramatic vistas of the Spanish Peaks framed by ten-foot-high windows. In the soaring, sun-drenched spaces, river stones piled to the ceilings become the walls, and the power of the masonry is equaled by the heft and scale of heroic columns, beams, and hanging king posts. Above the windows a gridded clerestory permits a higher sight line for the distant mountain view.

Throughout the interior, exaggerated details such as the giant joint pegs of the posts and beams and oversized whipstitching on leather upholstery underscore the scale established by the architecture. Texture and pattern are highlighted in the muted striations and artful shapes of the river rocks, in chunky slabs of Mojave bluestone paving floors and countertops, and in cushion covers stitched from Mexican blankets. Add a pair of tiered antler chandeliers, a duo of gnarled Thomas Molesworth settees, and a coffee table that doubles as a drum, and nothing else is needed to capture the sense of romance and boundless possibility embodied by the American West.

The porch of the ten thousand-square-foot cabin in southwestern Montana takes advantage of views toward the Spanish Peaks (above). A flat stone without the glitter of quartzite, Mojave bluestone paves the entrance hall (opposite), where tiered antlers make elegant chandeliers. Pine timbers from the Bitterroot Valley were hand peeled for texture.

About one hundred tons of hand-picked river rock
were used in the house, including the stones for
a shower adjacent to a bedroom chimney (above).
A load-bearing post-and-beam construction system
made a peaked wall of glass possible in the living
room (right). The vintage settees by Thomas
Molesworth were found by Helen Kent, the interior
designer. "We mixed in antiques to make the house
look like it had been lived in for years," she says.

HIGH-TECH RUSTIC

This elegant cluster of buildings grazing the shore of a New England lake is a work of art designed by and for nature—entwined with twigs and branches but resonating with a spirit greater than the sum of the physical parts. Inspired by turn-of-the-century Adirondack camps, the woodland retreat consists of three primary structures and outbuildings, all related by materials, siting, and stylistic features.

The architect Christopher Williams began the three-year project with a traditional boathouse including the customary upper-level game room and a porch overhanging the lake. The second phase was a four-bedroom, four-bath guest house with a kitchen, living and dining spaces, and a children's play area arranged in an open floor plan. The centerpiece of the camp, the main house, is a rambling lodge with two angled wings flanking a central two-story entry hall and Great Room. In this final structure, small, intimate nooks and corners play off large central spaces, and the forms of both furniture and architecture become lighter and more sophisticated.

"The intention was to design a building that was contemporary and even high tech," says Williams of the central lodge, "but it also had to have rustic overtones and look like a lake house that has been where it has been a long time." Each detail was carefully thought through. Several trees might be rejected before just the right bend of branches could be found; custom furnishings, overseen by the interior designer Mary Clark-Conley, were created to fit particular places in particular rooms; and a sophisticated computerized lighting system was installed.

Yet the buildings never seem contrived or overstated. A humanizing scale was achieved through varied roof pitches and a studied placement of walls, columns, and beams that creates a feeling of intimacy even in larger rooms. "The spaces are big, but we use every inch of them," says one of the owners, who revels in the feeling of openness that brings the outdoors right inside. Even more important is an underlying element of surprise: ribs of wall paneling that are really slender cattails, a piece of birch bark bearing an animal's claw marks. Such unexpected details startle and delight while they strike a note of familiarity that welcomes visitors and becomes the true soul of the camp.

The focal point of the main lodge is the two-story Great Room (opposite), designed as a rustic cathedral of light where glass expanses and white walls make it feel as open as possible. A copper chandelier in the entry (above) incorporates four separate circuits for uplighting, downlighting (through wildlife silhouettes), floodlighting, and twinkling sidelighting. In the dining room (pages 150–51), tables group into various formations and a bark sideboard lets window light flow through. A screened porch (page 151, top) leads to the adjacent kitchen (page 151, bottom).

Before designing this New England retreat, the owners and the architect toured historic Adirondack camps to study rustic craftsmanship and building techniques. Conceived in three phases, the project began with the boathouse (left bottom) so that lessons learned here could be passed on to the next structure. By the time work started on the guest house (above and opposite), artisans had improved their methods of peeling bark and piecing together "trees" from yellow birch. The main lodge (left top) was built last. After Christopher Williams, the architect, designed the lacy patterns for the gable decorations and balconies, the builders found twigs and branches to fit.

JUST A CABIN IN THE WOODS

Allan Skriloff favors honest, handsome rooms that do not try to be anything other than what they are. Can such spaces still be compelling? "Absolutely," says the New York artist and interior designer, whose own house in the Catskill Mountains bears out the point. The cabin, built of peeled red pine from Michigan, reflects Skriloff's proclivity for natural, "masculine" materials, but here the rugged timbers create spaces that seem uncluttered, clean, and up-to-date.

To set the stage, Skriloff created a conscious play of surfaces and scale. On entering the cabin, not a single log is to be seen. Smooth Sheetrock walls are painted a rich red, and the galvanized tin ceiling is kept purposely low. Walking into the Great Room, which sweeps upward twenty-eight feet, offers a transition from a small, confined space into a grand one. Substantial walls are laid in log from floor to ceiling. Underfoot is a pure expanse of maple flooring, while floating above is a snow-white ceiling. In this understated setting, the furniture has a strong presence. Custom-designed sofas set clean, pleasing profiles, and a mix of antiques and simple wood pieces, picked up at flea markets, holds its own with sculptural shapes.

Skriloff's house, an expression of his artistry, also fulfills his quest for privacy. He spent several years looking for the site, a wooded property of eight acres bordered by state land on three sides. No houses in the area are permitted to be seen from the road, and Skriloff's own appears only after a long approach down a winding driveway. The mature, forested landscape is dense with majestic old evergreens and masses of mountain laurel. Wildlife abounds, but neighbors do not, which is just the way he wants it. "You really feel like you are in the woods."

"Less is more," Allan Skriloff says of his minimalist design, in which textured logs contrast with clean wall surfaces (above). Massive pine timbers from Michigan and a plank door with strap hinges underscore a look of substance (opposite). With its tin roof and bright red walls, the front hall offers an unexpectedly warm welcome.

The open floor plan accommodates a living-dining area (opposite). Skriloff hand picked the birch flooring board by board to ensure that there would be no graining to fight with the pattern and texture of the log timbers. Radiant heat underfoot is augmented by an antique woodstove (above). The loft level contains the master bedroom (page 158, top). Carpeted for warmth, the room includes lamps Skriloff designed to fit the space. In the bath (page 158, bottom), an old copper tub from a flea market and wide plank floors create a traditional look. The artist's studio (pages 158–59) uses less formal spruce flooring to mark it as his workspace.

THE GREAT CAMP REINVENTED

Hovering on the edge of a pea-green marsh like a bird preparing for takeoff, this imposing hunting lodge is a complex structure layered with abstract patterning and laced through with provocative elements of irony and surprise. The twig-embellished house, hanging over the water on giant oak tree trunks, is the vacation residence of a serious hunter and accommodates his family's large guest parties during waterfowl season. In some ways the lodge, which sleeps up to twenty-two, resembles a comfortable private hotel. Symmetrical wings flanking a central tower and living room enclose a master suite and nursery as well as spaces for amusement and retreat: the gun, card, exercise, and game rooms traditional to the turn-of-the-century country gentleman's estate, as well as a movie theater, bar, and guest lounge.

Rustic stickwork, finishes, and furniture—and the custom of enormous hunting parties—hark back to the Gilded Age, but the design's self-conscious, edgy friction is rooted in modern abstract art. "It's really about a certain attitude and wit," comments the architect, Mark Simon, who perceives the fifteen-thousand-square-foot lodge as an Adirondack Great Camp reinvented. Although the building's wings are conventional rectangles, the spaces within are a jumble of volumes: inflected, telescoped, and backed uneasily into trapezoidal corners. Levels change and proportions invert. Trees appear to grow from one floor to another, and twiggy balusters stagger drunkenly down stairs. A catwalk creeps around the second story, while hidden passageways and two-way mirrors startle visitors at every turn.

The lodge's rustic aesthetic may appear inspired by nature, but it is quite carefully contrived. The interior bark finishes, tree work, and twigging are by the craftsman and furniture maker Daniel Mack. In nineteenth-century tradition he created a cottage industry of workers to assemble the materials, treated differently in each room. Limbs grow jaggedly over the living room ceiling, trees march down the sides of the game room, and branches spread into Gothic arches above the sky-blue guest lounge. Sometimes trees had to be pieced together to get the right configuration. But if in this attempt to recreate nature the builder's hand is obvious, that, says the architect, "is exactly the point."

At the entrance to the three-thousand-acre estate stands a pair of caretakers' houses that form the gatehouse. The two are linked by a bald eagle nesting in branches (above). The main lodge's central tower (opposite) is the architect's whimsical reference to lookout towers at Boy Scout camps. Posts rising out of the marsh are native white oak.

Twiggy branchwork forms a natural screen for windows offering views of the marsh and pine barren (left). "Branches" of stock-size pressure-treated pine sprout from oak tree trunks measuring two feet in diameter (above). Rope was coiled to camouflage the porch joints and stretched taut to make a railing.

A year before ground was broken, the craftsman Daniel Mack sent crews to forage from the Lower Hudson River north to the Adirondacks for just the right windblown trees and crooked branches for his interior finishes. Trees were shaped to create Gothic arches in the guest lounge (left). A dramatic

staircase (above) shows how angles and directions constantly change. Each stone was individually cut for the granite fireplace (right). "The idea was to expose the hand of man in the attempt to recreate nature," says the architect Mark Simon, a descendant of turn-of-the-century Adirondack camp owners.

Playing convex shapes off concave volumes, a curved hall (above) edges a circular dining room (opposite), where a sixty-foot mural by James Richmond depicts the local landscape in four seasons. The designer Mariette Himes Gomez added soft netting to a branch headboard (page 168). The Rube Goldberg–like faucet at a copper washtub sink (page 169, top left) is sensor activated. Guest quarters on the property (page 169, clockwise from top right) include an efficient bunkroom, a library, and a dressing hall.

A WALK IN THE FOREST

Just as a stroll through the woods unfolds in a progression of changing moods, textures, and light patterns, so does the passage between the rugged lodge and boathouse built by a young couple wishing to capture memories of childhoods spent in the Adirondacks. A ladderlike stair pitches from the lodge at the top of the hill to a rocky terrace framed by an outcropping of boulders. From here, jagged stone steps lead to a path that wanders along the contours of the incline, doubles back on itself, and finally arrives at the quizzical-looking boathouse at the water's edge.

Both lodge and boathouse, slightly off-center and covered in bark-covered pine, were commissioned from the architecture firm Bohlin Cywinski Jackson and consciously recall Adirondack Great Camp architecture. But they exhibit a contemporary quirkiness as well. The boathouse's tree-trunk posts cant out like elephants' legs, and twigs and brackets have a modern slant. To enter the main house one walks through a forest of peeled cedar-trunk columns into a large, open dining and living area, where the focal point is a mammoth fireplace piled high with round, muscular boulders. Rafters floating to a roof ridge seventeen feet high and the sheer size of the fireplace (page 35)—which descends to provide a second hearth in the children's quarters below—suggest the grand scale of the woods outside. Twiggy furnishings, feet splayed into roots, accent the Adirondack theme.

In the custom of the Great Camps of old, the project brought together local artisans, who collaborated on the complicated masonry, the furniture, and the evocative light fixtures of twig, glass, steel, and stretched rawhide. "We tried to identify with the craft of the region," says the architect Peter Bohlin, "but nothing's literal. The details are part of it, but the idea is to capture the sense of the thing." That sense comes ultimately through in the building's visible brotherhood with the forest, signaled in the rocky foundation emerging from the hill and tree trunks rising upward to a roof of lead-coated copper throwing off the blue light of the sky.

From the lodge atop a steep hill (above), a winding path leads to the lakeside boathouse (opposite). The two buildings recall early Great Camps with an Adirondack vocabulary of knotty bark, twig detailing, red trim, and deep roof overhangs.

Architectural elements do most of the decorating inside the main lodge, where rustic chairs and tables sit on bare floors (left). The dining room light fixture, designed by Peter Bohlin, is a single plane of opal glass. The supreme simplicity of the stairwell (above) reflects the influence of Japanese design.

BRANDENBURG CONCERTO

A certain poetry of material and form defines the work of David Salmela, the Minnesota architect who remodeled this quietly beautiful North Woods residence for the wildlife photographer Jim Brandenburg by adding a timber-framed guest house and studio spaces to an existing complex of cabins. Linked to one of the older buildings by a gallery and dining room, the new wing is placed opposite a garage and second studio. In this villagelike grouping by a courtyard, each structure becomes a comfortable neighbor to the next. A soothing geometry is echoed over again in the unbroken surfaces of lapboard roofs, in the perfect vertical columns of smooth brick chimneys, and even in the trim bands of grass and fine gravel surrounding the various buildings.

This composed Scandinavian spareness emerged as the architect's modernist sensibility melded with Brandenburg's desire to express the intuitive connection he feels to the building heritage of his ancestral Norway. Inspired by the functional form of a Viking longhouse, the main addition is an elongated 4,600-square-foot structure nudged into a hillside. The smallest of its three overlapping gable-roofed sections is a one-story room for camera storage. The central two-story space includes a guest sitting area and bedroom, and the last section, a three-story space to the southwest, layers a photography studio, computer balcony, and upper-level attic loft.

A studio and guest quarters at Ravenwood, the Minnesota home of Jim and Judy Brandenburg, are located in a longhouse distinguished by an elegant roof of lapped cedar and a decorative prow (right top). Broad glass expanses in the longhouse gallery (right bottom) frame a view of a second studio across the court.

Brandenburg was lured by the sheer remoteness of his property, which borders a three-million-acre forest and lake preserve straddling the Canadian border. "I love the raw nature and wilderness of it," the photographer says simply. Like a woodland creature, his house sits in the woods, waiting and watching. Reminiscent of traditional Norwegian buildings, Salmela's three-part addition appears organically attached to the terrain, camouflaged by the dark exterior stain and linked to the steep site by a screen of cedar planks and a stone wall. The flat sod roof covering the camera room is a clear reference to Scandinavian building custom, as are the vertical stave siding, steep roof pitches, and decorative ship's prow projecting from the last gable end.

However, the addition never becomes totally imitative, according to Salmela, who stresses that "it's the *emotional* connection that is important." To span the centuries without being too literal, the design pares both building and landscape to rudimentary elements that juxtapose old and new. On one hand, sculptural cairns and walls of taconite slabs laid dry into crumbling forms could be ancient remnants of the Stone Age. On the other, plate glass and minimalist interiors framed in fir and cedar strike a contemporary chord that heads the composition straight toward the new millennium. That sort of opposition, says Salmela, is both intentional and the basis of good design. "As the contradiction increases," asserts the architect, "so does the interest."

In the dining room (left top), the old cabin's original logs are stained white to contrast with the building's dark facades. The studio fireplace (left bottom), complete with stove, is tall enough for logs stacked vertically in the Scandinavian tradition. Ancient taconite slabs merge with a streamlined mantel of sleek steel.

In the loft guest room of the longhouse (opposite), steeply pitched, white-painted fir rafters rise in simple, perfect geometry to the ridge board. David Salmela's design for the house, which received an Honor Award from the American Institute of Architects, relies on the beauty of natural materials such as the cedar wall paneling and slate flooring. The bedroom stair (above) leads down to the photographer's computer loft (right top), where slatted platforms serve as open storage space. The studio (right bottom) is located on the level below.

STICK STYLE

Fishers Island is one of those quintessential New England summer colonies where neither the shingled houses nor the island itself has changed much in the last sixty years. But although tradition is strong here, every once in a while things get politely shaken up. Take this surprising beach house set on a windswept hill amid a good-natured snarl of brambles, oaks, and locust trees. For the architect, Leonard Wyeth, the weathered-shingle structure detailed with Gothic windows and "crazy quilt" stickwork represents the perfect cross between this Connecticut community's quiet gentility and the distinctive personality of his client, a young film producer who spent summers growing up on the island. "With her wonderful, eccentric sense of humor, she likes to view the quirks of the world," says Wyeth, "and she looks at everything with a calculating eye."

Approached from the west, the compact four-bedroom residence resembles a brood of small structures surrounding the mother house, all sharing a family resemblance in their cedar shingle siding, steep pitched roofs, and "drunken" stickwork. A series of freestanding gabled entry porches is designed to shade double glass doors from the summer sun.

The interior is just as playful, with a layout of cubical and elliptical spaces that read as a jumble of modern volumetric surprises. To avoid the accumulated paraphernalia so often found in summer houses, the owner has left the rooms deliberately, unashamedly bare. Interest comes from the clean, sculptural shapes and the shifting light over white walls. In this pared-down setting, tongue-in-cheek detailing such as the living room's stickwork cornice has more impact, and the house adopts a look of friendly spontaneity.

Made of stock framing lumber, a cornice of angled sticks in the living room—a playful twist on Adirondack twigwork—creates a good-natured surprise. "It's as if we put a bunch of sticks in a box," says the architect Leonard Wyeth, "and shook it up to see what would happen."

CATALOGUE

THE COMPANY STORE

Rustic Bridge

Cedar. 3′ high, 6′ long and larger. Romancing the Woods. Bridges (above) are available in custom sizes and a wide variety of styles. They are handcrafted from durable Eastern red cedar to ensure long life and service outdoors.

Summer House

Cedar. 10′ high, 12′ diameter. Romancing the Woods. Constructed of branches and trunks, this gazebo (below left) seats eight people and is handcrafted from aromatic red cedar to last a lifetime. Similar styles in a variety of sizes are also available.

Rustic Gate and Fence

Cedar. Romancing the Woods. Gates and fences (below right) are individually designed and sized to meet the client's specifications. Each item is crafted by hand from Eastern red cedar for durability.

Tandem Swing

Hardwood. 32″ high,
45″ wide, 30½″ deep.
Frame: 63½″ high,
57¼″ wide, 55″ deep.
No. 22171. L. L. Bean.
A swing (above left)
updates the classic style
with a tandem version.

Hampton Armchair

Teak. 39½″ high,
22″ wide, 17″ deep.
No. 416271. Smith and
Hawken. This chair
(below left) offers a
contoured back and
seat for comfort. Folds
for storage and features
rust-free brass fittings
for added stability.

Folding Adirondack

Oak or maple. Chair
40″ high, 29½″ wide,
36″ deep. Table 20½″
high, 19½″ wide, 18½″
deep. Various colors.
No. 10452. L. L. Bean.
A classic Adirondack-
style chair (above
center) comes with
an attached footrest
and a table and folds
flat for easy storage.

Classic Adirondack

Cedar. Chair 38″ high,
31″ wide, 34″ deep plus
footrest. Table 18½″
high, 20″ wide, 37″ long.
Nos. 417956, 2095. Smith
and Hawken. The pre-
ferred seating of the
Great Camps is updated
for comfort with a
matching footrest and
table (below right).

Adirondack to Assemble

Pine. 40″ high, 29½″
wide, 36″ deep. Home-
ward. Made of solid
Argentine pine, this
Adirondack chair
(above right) comes as
a set with a table. Some
assembly is required.

Widow's Chair
Apple wood. 56″ high, 27″ wide, 23″ deep. Don C. King. Hand-crafted with an imaginative spider-web and pitchfork design, the Widow's Chair (above left) features a seat of woven rawhide.

Zebra Bench
Maple and willow. 46″ high, 72″ wide, 32″ deep. Don C. King. A highly artistic combination of maple and willow form the animated bench (below left). Supple elkhide covers the seat.

Art Chair
Pine. 66″ high, 18″ wide, 18″ deep. No. C14-88. New West. Lodgepole pine legs contrast with the contorted and twisting features of burl wood to form a unique rendition of a high-back chair (above center). The padded seat has a wool Chimayo weaving.

Lilac Arm Chair
Lilac and maple. 51″ high, 28″ wide, 27″ deep. Adirondack Rustics Gallery. The vivid grain of curly maple forms the seat of this arm chair (above right). Lilac twists and curves to form the legs, angled back, and arms.

Gothic Root Throne
Rhododendron roots. Various sizes. Jerry and Jessica Farrell. This handcrafted rustic throne (below right), fashioned from very old roots and burls, takes on a living, rustic quality all its own.

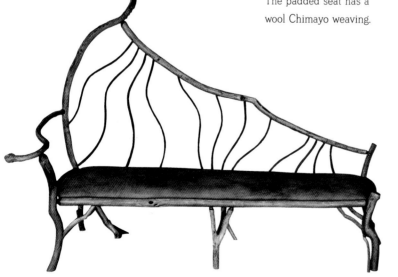

Tête-à-Tête Loveseat

Willow and maple. 48″
high, 60″ long, 34″ deep.
Sleeping Bear Twig
Furniture. Shoots of
bent willow form the
graceful arches of this
loveseat (above).

Three-Arch Rocker

Willow and oak.
48″ high, 32″ wide,
34″ deep. Sleeping
Bear Twig Furniture.
Sturdy oak provides
support for this rocker
with a triple-arch
back (below). Custom
orders are accepted.

High-Back Throne

Willow and maple.
72″ high, 30″ wide,
30″ deep. Sleeping Bear
Twig Furniture. Willow
sweeps over the back
and top of this high-
back chair (right) to
form a rustic throne.

Colored Twig Bench

Willow, birch, and dogwood. 38″ high, 45″ wide, 22″ deep. Rustic Furniture. Hundreds of small twigs combine to create a mosaic effect on the bench (above left). Handcrafted with a geometric pattern on the back of the chair.

Steerhead Ranch Chairs

Pine. 33″ high, 25″ wide, 24″ deep. No. C16-191A. New West. Western-look arm chairs (below left) have a pine frame and lodgepole legs with a burl spreader. A relief carving on the back complements the upholstered leather, which is fixed with brass studs.

Morris Adjustable Chair

Hickory. 42″ high, 25″ wide, 44″ deep. Old Hickory Furniture Company. A rustic interpretation of the classic Morris chair (above center) comes in a wide variety of upholstery options.

Burl-Leg Club Chairs

Pine and alder. 33″ high, 35″ wide, 38″ deep. No. CC10-69. New West. Pine poles are applied on the chair's upholstered alder frame (below right), with a choice of burl or knee legs. Red leather is accented with a Chimayo weaving on the back.

Hoop Settee

Hickory. 36″ high, 57″ wide, 27″ deep. No. 140-45. Old Hickory Furniture Company. Made with handcrafted hickory wood and hand caning, the piece (above right) continues the company's long tradition of rustic furniture.

Canoe Coffee Table

Cedar and mahogany.
18″ high, 60″ wide,
16″ deep. No. 18384.
L. L. Bean. Handcrafted
from white cedar and
mahogany with genuine
cedar ribs and gun-
wales, the table (above
left) is finished with
brass fittings and a
rawhide woven seat
for authenticity.

Antler Table

Antlers. 18″ high,
30″ diameter. No. TA135.
Arte de Mexico.
A rounded ½″-thick
glass top is supported
by a base of naturally
shed antlers (below
left). The glass top
is available in chiseled,
beveled, and polished
variations.

Birch-Bark Side Table

Fir, birch, and willow.
30″ high, 48″ wide,
15″ deep. Sleeping Bear
Twig Furniture. Bent
willow branches add
grace to the table
(below center), high-
lighted with cedar bark
on the top and sides.

Pole-Leg Table

Pine, maple, and birch.
30″ high, 48″ diameter.
No. T28. New West. Four
curved lodgepole pine
legs support this table
(above right) with an
applied pole edge
around the circular
table top, which features
alternating sections of
maple, birch, and pine.

Lilac End Table

Lilac and birch.
26″ high, 15″ diameter.
Adirondack Rustics
Gallery. A birch burl
forms the table top
(below right), which
undulates around the
legs of lilac. They twist
and bend as they rise
to support the burl top.

Burl-Leg Buffet

Birch and pine. 34" high, 50" wide, 20" deep. No. CW56. New West. Carved elk and deer appear on the pine doors (above). The legs and details are burl, and the top is leather, fixed with brass studs.

Buffalo Bill Credenza

Willow, birch, and pine. 30" high, 50" wide, 26" deep. New West. Handpainted and hand-carved images of Buffalo Bill adorn the sugar pine doors of the credenza (below). Under a rawhide top, both drawers feature rawhide fronts and antler pulls.

Corner China Cabinet

Birch and pine. 95" high, 40" wide, 34" deep. No. CW52. New West. Beetle-tracked Ponderosa pine trim accents the birch carcass wood of the cabinet (right), which features glass shelves and antler door pulls.

Twig Chest

Willow. 32" high,
45" wide, 20" deep.
Rustic Furniture. Crafted
using precisely cut twigs
inlaid in a symmetrical
pattern on both door
fronts, the chest is
mosaiclike (above left).

Wormwood Dresser

Birch and pine.
54" high, 38" wide, 24"
deep. No. CW60. New
West. This wormwood
dresser (below left)
features beetle-tracked
pine trim and a leather
top, sides, and drawers.

Painted Highboy

Pine. 72" high, 48" wide,
18" deep. No. CW12-93.
New West. Ponderosa
pine trim and details
surround an original oil
painting by Lana Peratti
in front (below center).

Rustic Dresser

Birch and dogwood.
32" high, 26" wide, 20"
deep. Rustic Furniture.
A handcrafted dresser
(above right) features
two drawers with fronts
of inlaid twigs and a
wall mirror to match.

Lodgepole Pine Bureau

Birch and pine.
38" high, 40" wide,
24" deep. No. CW11-22.
New West. Lodgepole is
applied on birch, while
sides and drawers sport
red leather (below right).

Antler Mirror
Antlers. 44″ high, 26″ wide, 8″ deep. No. MF-100. Arte de Mexico. A graceful oval of antlers forms the frame of the wall mirror (above left). Only naturally shed antlers are used for the company's furnishings.

Manzanita Bed
Manzanita and pine. 6′ high, 65″ wide, 100″ long. Rocky Mountain Timber Products. The bed uses manzanita and pine that has been debarked and finely sanded (below left).

Twig Frame Mirror
White birch. 37″ high, 22″ wide. Nick Nickerson. This frame (above center) is fashioned from twigs of varying length. The artist specializes in one-of-a-kind designs that are meant to be unique items for each client.

Juniper Bed
Juniper. 6′ high, 65″ wide, 110″ long. Rocky Mountain Timber Products. High-altitude juniper wood writhes and twists to form a unique bed frame (below right). Beds are shipped disassembled.

Bass Wall Mirror
Birch bark. 56″ high, 37″ wide. Nick Nickerson. This mirror (above right) uses twigs and a mounted bass for an artful composition.

Rustic Mantel Clock

Birch. 16″ high, 25″ wide, 12″ deep. Jerry and Jessica Farrell. Made from birch bark and twigs, a rustic mantel clock (above) features a symmetrical pattern. The clock face includes an oil painting by Jessica Farrell.

Bear Mantel Clock

Composite. 11″ high, 12″ wide, 5″ deep. No. 60561. Plow and Hearth. Designed to evoke the spirit of classic lodge clocks (below), this one keeps accurate time with a battery-powered quartz movement.

Bear Case Clock

Willow. 6½′ high, 20″ wide, 15″ deep. Jerry and Jessica Farrell. Precisely cut twigs create a tall case clock (right). Twigs alternate in color for rich geometric patterns. The front panel and face feature a Jessica Farrell oil painting.

Antler Floor Lamp
Antlers. 65″ high, 28″ diameter. No. FL1009. Arte de Mexico. An antler base rises to support an elegant, lacy floor lamp (left) made from antlers that are shed naturally.

Antler Chandelier
Antlers. 36″ high, 48″ diameter. No. CH597. Arte de Mexico. A weaving of antlers holds eight lights (above). Shades are separate.

Bison Lamp
Antlers. 18″ high, 8″ wide. No. HF040. J. Marco Galleries. Handcrafted from natural antlers, this lamp (below) features a hand-painted leather shade depicting a bison. The pull switch is antler.

Birch Lamp and Shade
Birch. Lamp 21″ high.
Shade 10½″ high, 14″
wide. Nos. 135J7, 135H7.
Whispering Pines. This
birch-bark lamp (below
left) is available in
smaller sizes and with a
variety of scenic shades.

Buffalo Hunt Chandelier
Steel and rawhide. 54″
high, 36″ diameter. No.
S3-38A. New West. Cut
steel forms the frame of
the chandelier (above
left), featuring a painted
rawhide lodge and
shield and buffalo skull
and arrow hanger rods.

Fish Lamp
Pine. Various sizes.
Amber Jean. Crafted
from old pine fence
posts and handpainted
by the artist, these have
copper shades by Joseph
Franklin (below center).

Antler Sconce
Antlers. 10″ high, 21″
wide, 8″ deep. No. WM
129. Arte de Mexico.
This wall mount (above
right) is crafted from
antlers that support
two lights. Shades are
not included but may
be ordered separately.

Bear Lamp
Steel. 9″ high, 12″
diameter. No. 6271.
Plow and Hearth. A
hand-stenciled bear and
forest design is on the
shade, above a powder-
coated, rust-finished
steel base (below right).

Moose Key Plaque
Steel. 7" high, 12" wide. No. HD165. J. Marco Galleries. This hand-cut steel plaque features a moose design, sealed for durability (above left). Keys can hang from seven hooks.

Bear Fireback
Iron. 15" high, 20" wide. No. 1580. Plow and Hearth. This cast-iron fireback (below left) will improve a fire's efficiency by reflecting heat back into a room.

Pinecone Lantern
Brass. 7¼" high. No. H66290. Coldwater Creek. Illuminated by a tea-light candle, the lantern (below center) shines through a pinecone and needle design cutout. Includes a handle for carrying.

Weathervane Ornaments
Metal. 3" high, 4" wide, 4" deep. Nos. 43C7, 43A7. Whispering Pines. Ornaments come with a verdigris finish and are styled after antique fixtures (above right).

Fire Bellows
Leather and wood. No. 1581. Plow and Hearth. Old-fashioned bellows (below right) help a roaring fire get started in seconds. Available either painted or with a clear finish.

Cabin Pillows

Cotton. 12″ long, 12″ wide. Nos. 88B7, 88A7. Whispering Pines. Chenille yarn adds texture and a rustic greeting to two versions of a soft cotton velvet pillow (above).

Adirondack Hooked Rug

Wool. 2′ long, 3′ wide. No. XD455E. Orvis. Hand-hooked rug (below) designed by Nancy Aitken features a playful forest theme and adds a woodsy touch as either a rug or a wall hanging.

Trapper Blankets

Wool (mothproofed). Twin, full, queen, and king sizes. No. 11375. L. L. Bean. 100% percent virgin New Zealand wool provides superior warmth (right) in these classic cabin coverings.

Twig Picture Frame

Red birch. 26″ high, 27″ wide. Nick Nickerson. This picture frame (above left) is made of various-sized twigs and shoots in a square pattern to create a balanced composition. Each frame is a unique creation by the artist.

Carved Picture Frames

Wood. 12″ high, 14″ wide or 9″ high, 11″ wide. Nos. 65A6, 64A6. Whispering Pines. These intricately handcarved frames (below left) hold an 8-by-10″ or a 5-by-7″ photograph respectively.

Bent-Branch Frame

White birch. 13″ high, 17″ wide. Nick Nickerson. Bent branches seem to expand outward from the surface of the rectangular frame (above center). All of this artist's frames are individual commissions and come with nostalgic prints.

Rusticated Frames

Wood. 10″ high, 11½″ wide. Nos. 150B6, 150C6. Whispering Pines. Each rusticated picture frame (below right) holds a 4-by-6″ photograph. Available in a variety of rustic themes and colors.

Birch-Bark Frame

Birch with red birch trim. 23″ high, 25″ wide. Nick Nickerson. Crafted from the classic material used in Adirondack goods, the frame (above right) has a wonderfully varied texture and colors that range from black to a soft white.

Trout Lake Utensils
Metal. Nos. 74A6, 75A6.
Whispering Pines.
A large spoon and fork
offer a rustic way to
serve the day's catch
(below left). Also
available in a smaller
three-piece set with a
knife. Great for picnics
or dining in the wilds.

Trout Platter
Tempered glass. 14″
oval. No. 92A7. Whisper-
ing Pines. Delightful
patterns and graphics
combine on this
découpaged glass
platter (above). Not
suitable for dishwasher.

Fish Salad Servers
Wood. 11¼″ long.
No. H67777. Coldwater
Creek. Handmade
servers (below right)
are fashioned from
wood and feature
painted fish handles.
Ample-sized fork and
spoon handle salads
with ease. Servers are
not dishwasher safe.

Carved Bear with Fish
Pine. 3′ high.
No. XK055F. Orvis.
Handcarved from solid
Ponderosa pine, this
bear statue (left)
makes a warm addition
to a covered porch or
inside the house. Comes
complete with fish.

SUPPLIERS

Adirondack Rustics Gallery
R.R. 1, Box 88
Charley Hill Road
Schroon Lake, N.Y. 12870
518-532-9384

Arte de Mexico
5356 Riverton Avenue
North Hollywood, Calif. 91601
818-508-0993

L. L. Bean
Freeport, Maine 04033
800-221-4221

Coldwater Creek
One Coldwater Creek Drive
Sandpoint, Idaho 83864
800-262-0040

Jerry and Jessica Farrell
P.O. Box 255
Sidney Center, N.Y. 13839
607-369-4916

Homeward
1007 Wisconsin Avenue, N.W.
Washington, D.C. 20007
800-616-3667

Amber Jean
1106 West Park
No. 268
Livingston, Mont. 59047
406-222-9251

Don C. King
HC 67
Box 2079
Challis, Idaho 83226
208-838-2449

J. Marco Galleries
758 Medina Road
Medina, Ohio 44256
800-948-3100

New West
2811 Big Horn Avenue
Cody, Wyo. 82414
307-587-2839

Nick Nickerson
P.O. Box 618
Copake, N.Y. 12516
518-329-1664

Old Hickory
Furniture Company
403 South Noble Street
Shelbyville, Ind. 46176
800-232-2275

Orvis
Historic Route 7A
Manchester, Vt. 05254
800-541-3541

Plow and Hearth
P.O. Box 5000
Madison, Va. 22727
800-627-1712

Rocky Mountain
Timber Products
P.O. Box 1477
Sisters, Ore. 97759
541-549-1322

Romancing the Woods
33 Raycliffe Drive
Woodstock, N.Y. 12498
914-246-6976

Rustic Furniture
10 Cloninger Lane
Bozeman, Mont. 59715
406-586-3746

Sleeping Bear
Twig Furniture
5711 Rice Road
Cedar, Mich. 49621
616-228-6633

Smith and Hawken
2 Arbor Lane
Box 6900
Florence, Ky. 41022
800-776-3336

Whispering Pines
39 Edward Street
P.O. Box 382
Sparkill, N.Y. 10976
800-836-4662

Wood Classics
Box 98A
Gardiner, N.Y. 12525
914-255-5599

With a deep, angled seat and wide arms for a writing pad or a drink, sturdy slatted chairs like these, designed in the late nineteenth century for rustic Adirondack camps, have become outdoor standards. This pair (no. 2013) from Wood Classics comes in mahogany or teak, assembled or in a kit (39½" high, seat 20" wide, 19" deep). A matching footrest (no. 2105) echoes the chair's lines.

CAMPING IN

LODGES FOR HIRE

Ahwahnee Hotel
Yosemite National Park
Yosemite, Calif. 95389
209-252-4848

Big Cedar Lodge
612 Devil's Pool Road
Ridgedale, Mo. 65739
417-335-2777

Crater Lake Lodge
P.O. Box 128
Crater Lake, Ore. 97604
503-830-8700

D'Amour's Big Cedar Lodge
P.O. Box 58
Lake Delton, Wis. 53940
608-254-8456

El Tovar Hotel
One Main Street
Grand Canyon, Ariz. 86023
520-638-2631

Fence Lake Lodge
12919 Frying Pan Camp Lane
Lac du Flambeau, Wis. 54538
888-588-3255

Garland Lodge
Box 364-M
County Road 489
Lewiston, Mich. 49756
800-968-0042

Glendorn
Bradford, Pa.
c/o Resorts Management
International
The Carriage House
201½ East 29th Street
New York, N.Y. 10016
212-696-4566

Gunflint Lodge
143 South Gunflint Lake
Grand Marais, Minn. 55604
800-328-3325

Henry's Fork Lodge
P.O. Box 600
Island Park, Idaho 83429
208-558-7953

Jenny Lake Lodge
P.O. Box 240
Moran, Wyo. 83013
307-733-4647

Lake Placid Lodge
Whiteface Inn Road
P.O. Box 550
Lake Placid, N.Y. 12946
518-523-2700

Little St. Simons Island
P.O. Box 21078
St. Simons Island, Ga. 31522
912-638-7472

Old Faithful Inn
TW Recreational Services
P.O. Box 165
Yellowstone National Park,
Wyo. 82190
307-344-7311

Placid Lake Log Cabin
c/o Property Management
of Hayward
P.O. Box 13113
Hayward, Wis. 54843
715-634-3565

The Point
P.O. Box 65
Saranac Lake, N.Y. 12983
518-891-5674

Red Setter Inn
P.O. Box 133
Greer, Ariz. 85927
520-735-7441

Salish Lodge
P.O. Box 1109
Snoqualmie, Wash. 98065
800-826-6124

Seven Lakes Lodge
738 County Road 59
Meeker, Colo. 81641
970-878-4772

Sundance
R.R. 3, Box A-1
Sundance, Utah 84604
801-225-4107

Timberline Lodge
Timberline Ski Area
Timberline Lodge, Ore. 97028
503-231-5400

Wawbeek Lodge
553 Panther Mountain Road
Tupper Lake, N.Y. 12986
518-359-2656

An Ozark retreat of grand porportions and rustic sensibility, Big Cedar Lodge in Missouri began as a pair of adjoining vacation retreats built in the 1920s. One of the houses was a log mansion with peeled-pole balconies and branchwork recalling the design of Adirondack lodges. Today guests are welcome at three main lodge buildings, forty individual cabins, and a conference center.

DESIGNERS

ARCHITECTS

Jeff Balch, Arcus Design Group, Exton, Pa.: pp. 34–35

Peter Bohlin, Bohlin Cywinski Jackson, Philadelphia, Pa.: pp. 35, 110–11, 170–73

Donald Breimhurst, Home Field Advantage, Ltd., St. Peter's, Pa.: pp. 118–23

Design Associates Architects, Jackson, Wyo.: pp. 26–27

John Diamond, Babcock Design Group, Salt Lake City, Utah: pp. 132–35

Jonathan Foote, Livingston, Mont., and Jackson, Wyo.: pp. 96–101 (restoration)

Richard Giegengack, Washington, D.C.: pp. 50–55 (new additions)

Jerry Locati, Bozeman, Mont.: pp. 144–47

Darryl Charles McMillan, Ketchum, Idaho: pp. 128–31

David Salmela, Duluth, Minn.: pp. 174–79

Mark Simon, Centerbrook Architects, Centerbrook, Conn.: pp. 29 left, 30–31, 33 right, 160–69

Candace Tillotson-Miller, Livingston, Mont.: front jacket, pp. 27, 32, 41, 136–43

Christopher Williams, Meredith, N.H.: pp. 28, 72–77 (restoration), 78–85 (restoration), 148–53

Leonard Wyeth, Centerbrook Architects, Centerbrook, Conn.: pp. 180–81

ARTISANS

Roc Corbett, Big Fork, Mont.: p. 34 (chandelier)

Peter Fillerup, Heber, Utah: pp. 36, 98–99, 130 (chandeliers)

Dimitri Gerakaris, North Canaan, N.H.: p. 28 (iron fireplace screen)

Daniel Mack, Warwick, N.Y.: pp. 30–31, 33 right, 160–69 (all rustic work)

Jack McNamara, Sun Valley, Idaho: pp. 128–31 (adobe masonry)

A. J. Obara Jr., Unionville, Pa.: pp. 112, 115 (sculpture)

Unique Timber Corporation, Lumby, B.C.: pp. 30, 33 top (stair)

ARTISTS

Sarah Horan, Toad Hall, Fly Creek, N.Y.: p. 40

James Richmond, New York, N.Y.: p. 166

BUILDERS

Alpine Log Homes, Victor, Mont.: pp. 34–35, 124–27

B K Cypress Log Homes, Bronson, Fla.: p. 6

Laabs and Associates, Bigfork, Montana: pp. 26–27

LaChance Builders, Whitefish, Mont.: pp. 34–35

Lok-n-Logs, Sherburne, N.Y.: pp. 2–3

Maple Island Log Homes, Suttons Bay, Mich.: pp. 50–55 (new additions), 118–23

Montana Log Homes, Kalispell, Mont.: p. 29 right, back jacket

Craig Reichstetter, Big Sky, Mont.: pp. 144–47

Rocky Mountain Log Homes, Hamilton, Mont.: pp. 36, 201

Sugarloaf Mountain Log Homes, Sugarloaf, Pa.: p. 39

Yellowstone Traditions, Bozeman, Mont.: pp. 27, 32, 41, 136–143

FURNITURE MAKERS

Barney Bellinger, Sampson Bog Studio, Mayfield, N.Y.: p. 51

Jerry and Jessica Farrell, Sidney Center, N.Y.: p. 67

Ken Heitz, Hamilton, N.Y.: p. 71

Old Hickory Furniture Company, Shelbyville, Ind.: p. 36

Pump and Circumstance, Eureka Springs, Ark.: pp. 38–39, 90

PHOTOGRAPHERS

Adirondack Museum: endleaves, pp. 12, 13, 18, 19 top, 20 bottom

Michel Arnaud: pp. 37 right, 132–33, 134–35, 135 right

Karl A. Backus, courtesy Bohlin Cywinski Jackson: pp. 35 right, 110–11, 170, 171, 172–73, 173 right

Jim Brandenburg: pp. 174–75 top, 176–77 bottom

Colorado Historical Society: p. 15

Jack Deo: p. 21 both

Nathan Farb: pp. 4–5

Bernard Handzel: pp. 154, 155, 156, 157, 158 top left and bottom, 158–59

Timothy Hursley: pp. 180–81

Bruce Katz: pp. 10–11, 19 bottom, 46–47, 48 left, 48–49

Peter Kerze: pp. 174–75 bottom, 176–77 top, 178, 179 all

Brian Lloyd: pp. 30 left, 33 left

Steven Mays: pp. 66, 67, 68 all, 69, 70, 71

Norman McGrath: pp. 1, 29 left, 30–31, 33 right, 160, 161, 162–63, 163 right, 164 left, 164–65, 165 right, 166, 167, 168, 169 all

Emily Minton, courtesy Rogers-Ford: pp. 8–9, 44–45, 50–51, 52–53, 54–55, 55 right

David M. Morris: p. 16

Randall Perry: casewrap, pp. 24–25, 56, 57, 58 left, 58–59, 60, 61, 62–63, 63 right, 64 left, 64–65

Fred Pflughoft: pp. 14 top, 17

Fred Pflughoft and **David M. Morris:** pp. 14 bottom, 22, 23

Paul Rocheleau, courtesy Maple Island Log Homes: pp. 118, 119, 120 left, 120–21, 122, 123

Rocky Mountain Log Homes: pp. 36, 201

Cheryle St. Onge: pp. 28, 37 left, 72, 73, 74–75, 75 right, 76, 77, 78–79, 80 left, 80–81, 82, 83 both, 84, 85, 148, 149, 150–51, 151 top right and bottom, 152 all, 153

Brad Simmons: pp. 2, 3, 38–39, 39 right, 40 both, 86, 87, 88–89, 89 right, 90, 91, 92, 93, 94, 95, 203

Superior View: p. 20 top

Roger Wade: jacket (front and back), pp. 6, 7, 26–27, 27 right, 29 right, 32, 34–35, 41, 42, 43, 96, 97, 98–99, 99 right, 100, 101 all, 102, 103, 104, 105, 106, 107, 108 left, 108–109, 124, 125, 126, 127, 128, 129, 130 all, 131, 136, 137, 138, 139 both, 140–41, 141 right, 142, 143 all, 144, 145, 146 left, 146–47

Whispering Pines: p. 208

Wood Classics: p. 198

Joel Zarska: pp. 112, 113, 114, 115, 116, 117

SELECTED BIBLIOGRAPHY

Barnes, Christine. *Great Lodges of the West*. Bend, Ore.: W. W. West, 1997.

Brimmer, F. E. *Camps, Log Cabins, Lodges and Clubhouses*. New York: D. Appleton—Century, 1937.

Bruette, William, ed. *Log Camps and Cabins: How to Build and Furnish Them (By Practical Campers and Woodsmen)*. Nessmark Library, 1934.

Comstock, Edward, ed. *The Adirondack League Club, 1890–1990*. Old Forge, N.Y., 1990.

Eckert, Kathryn Bishop. *Buildings of Michigan*. Buildings of the United States. Society of Architectural Historians. New York: Oxford University Press, 1993.

Flood, Elizabeth Clair. *Cowboy High Style: Thomas Molesworth to the New West*. Layton, Utah: Gibbs Smith, 1992.

Fox, Stephen. *John Muir and His Legacy: The American Conservation Movement*. Boston: Little, Brown, 1981.

Gilborn, Craig. *Adirondack Furniture and the Rustic Tradition*. New York: Harry N. Abrams, 1987.

————. *Durant: The Fortunes and Woodland Camps of a Family in the Adirondacks*. Blue Mountain Lake, N.Y.: Adirondack Museum, 1981.

Kaiser, Harvey. *Great Camps of the Adirondacks*. Boston: David R. Godine, 1982.

Kilborn, Robert. "Summer Colony Development." *American Architect* 143, no. 2618 (July 1933): 70–80.

Landau, Sarah Bradford. "Richard Morris Hunt: The Continental Picturesque, and the 'Stick Style.'" *Journal of the Society of Architectural Historians* 42, no. 3 (October 1983): 272–89.

Lane, Charles Stuart. *New Hampshire's First Tourists in the Lakes and Mountains*. Meredith, N.H.: Old Print Barn, 1993.

Mayhew, Edgar deN., and Minor Meyers Jr. *A Documentary History of American Interiors*. New York: Charles Scribner's Sons, 1980.

Mitchell, Lee Clark. *Witnesses to a Vanishing America: The Nineteenth-Century Response.* Princeton, N.J.: Princeton University Press, 1981.

National Collection of Fine Arts. *National Parks and the American Landscape.* Washington, D.C.: Smithsonian Institution, 1972.

National Park Service. *Architecture in the Parks: National Historic Landmark Theme Study*. Washington, D.C.: National Park Service, U.S. Department of the Interior, 1986.

————. *Park Structures and Facilities*. Washington, D.C.: National Park Service, U.S. Department of the Interior, 1935.

Rydholm, C. Fred. *Superior Heartland: A Backwoods History*. Vols. 1 and 11. Marquette, Mich., 1989.

Schneider, Paul. *The Adirondacks: A History of America's First Wilderness*. New York: Henry Holt, 1997.

Shepard, Augustus D. *Camps in the Woods*. New York: Architectural Book Publishing, 1931.

Shurtleff, Harold R. *The Log Cabin Myth*. 1939. Reprint, Gloucester, Mass.: Peter Smith, 1967.

Wheaton, Rodd L. "Rustic Connotations: Furnishing National Park Hostelries." In *Victorian Resorts and Hotels: Essays from a Victorian Society Autumn Symposium*. Victorian Society in America, 1992.

Wicks, William S. *Log Cabins: How to Build and Furnish Them*. New York: Forest and Stream Publishing, 1889.

Wilson, Richard Guy. "Nineteenth Century American Resorts and Hotels." In *Victorian Resorts and Hotels: Essays from a Victorian Society Autumn Symposium*. Victorian Society in America, 1992.

INDEX

SIMON & SCHUSTER EDITIONS

Rockefeller Center
1230 Avenue of the Americas
New York, N.Y. 10020

Manufactured in Singapore

10 9 8 7 6 5 4 3 2

**Produced by Archetype Press, Inc.,
Washington, D.C.**
Diane Maddex, Project Director
Gretchen Smith Mui, Editor
John Hovanec, Editorial Assistant
Robert L. Wiser, Designer

Endpapers: Guests on the porch
at Santanoni, a Great Camp
in the Adirondacks of New York.
(Adirondack Museum)

Page 1: New cabin at a modern-
day Great Camp along the East
Coast. (© Norman McGrath)

Pages 2–3: Winter and summer
views of a cabin in Cooperstown,
N.Y. (© Brad Simmons)

Pages 4–5: Lake Placid, located
in the six-million-acre Adirondack
State Park. (© Nathan Farb)

Page 6: Porch of the Andresen
residence in Archer, Florida.
(© Roger Wade)

Pages 8–9: The staircase at
Topridge, Marjorie Merriweather
Post's Adirondack retreat. (Emily
Minton, courtesy Rogers-Ford)

Pages 202–3: Looking out the
Stearns cabin in Sommersville, Ky.
(© Brad Simmons)

Page 208: Metal lamp from the
Whispering Pines catalogue.
(Whispering Pines)

**Library of Congress
Cataloging-in-Publication Data**
Carley, Rachel.
Cabin fever : rustic style comes
home / Rachel Carley.
p.   cm.
"An Archetype Press book."
Includes bibliographical
references and index.
1. Log cabins—United States.
2. Camps—United States.
3. Vernacular architecture—
United States. 4. Decoration and
ornament, Rustic—United States.
I. Title.
NA8470.C35 1998   98-21134
728.7'3'0973—dc21   CIP

A Note on the Typography
The text of this book was typeset
in Meyer Two, originally produced
in 1926 by Linotype for the Hollywood mogul Louis B. Mayer and
revived in 1994 by David Berlow
for the Font Bureau. The display
typeface is Greco Adornado,
produced in 1925 by Gans and
revived in 1992 by the Lazy Dog
Type Foundry as Greco Deco.